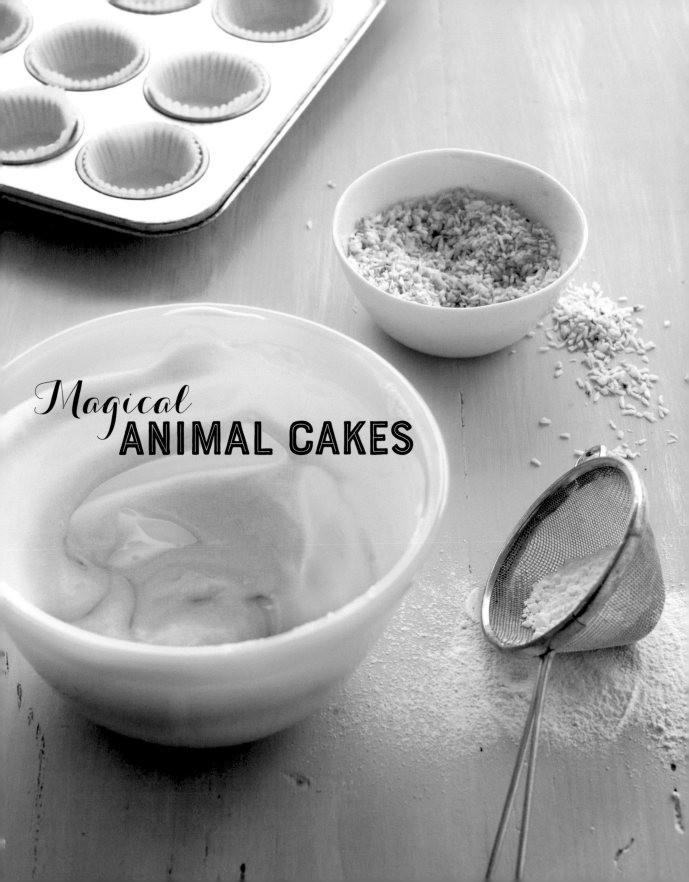

Magical
ANIMAL CAKES

Magical ANIMAL CAKES

45 bakes for unicorns, sloths, llamas and other cute critters

ANGELA ROMEO
& ANNIE RIGG

RYLAND PETERS & SMALL
LONDON • NEW YORK

Senior Designer Toni Kay
Editor Sarah Vaughan
Production Manager Gordana Simakovic
Art Director Leslie Harrington
Editorial Director Julia Charles
Publisher Cindy Richards
Indexer Stephen Blake

First published in 2020 by
Ryland Peters & Small
20–21 Jockey's Fields, London
WC1R 4BW
and
341 E 116th St, New York NY 10029
www.rylandpeters.com

10 9 8 7 6 5 4 3 2 1

Recipe collection compiled by
Sarah Vaughan

ISBN: 978-1-78879-191-5

Printed in China

A CIP record for this book is available
from the British Library.

US Library of Congress Cataloging-in-
Publication Data has been applied for.

NOTES:
• Both British (Metric) and American
(Imperial plus US cups) measurements
are included in these recipes for your
convenience, however it is important
to work with one set of measurements
and not alternate between the two
within a recipe.
• All spoon measurements are level
unless otherwise specified. A teaspoon
is 5 ml, a tablespoon is 15 ml.
• All eggs are medium (UK) or large
(US), unless specified as large, in which
case US extra-large should be used.
Uncooked or partially cooked eggs
should not be served to the very old, frail,
young children, pregnant women or those
with compromised immune systems.
• Ovens should be preheated to the
specified temperatures. We recommend
using an oven thermometer. If using a
fan-assisted oven, adjust temperatures
according to the manufacturer's
instructions.
• When a recipe calls for the grated
zest of citrus fruit, buy unwaxed fruit and
wash well before using. If you can only
find treated fruit, scrub well in warm
soapy water before using.

CONTENTS

INTRODUCTION

Top off a themed birthday party with the ultimate animal cake and have baking requests covered with this book full of magical designs. There's a creation for everyone - from a fabulous two-tier Tropical Flamingo to a roarsome King of the Jungle Lion - perfect for little imaginations as well as for all the big kids at heart!

As you make your way through the animal cakes, cookies and more, you'll discover a wealth of clever tricks and short cuts, such as candies and chocolates for eyes, and liquorice strips for tongues and tails! Enjoy exploring different decorating techniques with these creative animal bakes - try a touch of fondant icing, test out the smooth, shiny results of flood icing and enjoy experimenting with the versatile nature of buttercream.

This collection of recipes is great for building your cakey-confidence. We hope you have fun recreating these magical recipes - you'll see how the decorating techniques can be transferred to any design you or your little ones can dream up. There are classic cake mixtures in differing sizes and with easily adjustable flavours - the Basic Vanilla Cake can be easily converted into delicious chocolate, lemon or orange. The possibilities are endless to personalise to your own preferred taste.

When juggling goodie bags, sandwiches, gifts and invitations, you'll also want to enjoy your time spent cake decorating! So choose a design to match the time you have, and plan ahead by making any pieces that you can in advance. Finally, enjoy the smiles then the satisfied peace when everyone is eating the tasty results!

Angela x

BASIC *Recipes*

BASIC VANILLA CAKE

This is the most basic vanilla cake mixture, which can be adapted to introduce different flavours, such as chocolate (see end of recipe). It is used in many of the recipes in this book as it makes a good base for cakes that need to be cut up and re-assembled, and it tends to be liked by most of the family, young and old. Here there are four quantities to suit individual recipes but the method remains the same regardless of the quantity you use. For best results use an electric freestanding mixer, but a hand-held electric whisk will do just fine. Before you start baking make sure all the ingredients are at room temperature, the oven is preheated with the oven shelf in the correct position and the relevant cake pans have been prepared. The oven temperatures given throughout the book are for a conventional oven; if you are using a fan oven, adjust the temperature according to the manufacturer's instructions.

EXTRA LARGE

350 g/3 sticks unsalted butter,
   at room temperature
350 g/1^3/$_4$ cups caster/superfine sugar
6 large eggs, beaten
2 teaspoons pure vanilla extract
350 g/2^2/$_3$ cups plain/all-purpose flour
2^1/$_2$ teaspoons baking powder
4–5 tablespoons milk,
   at room temperature

LARGE

250 g/2^1/$_4$ sticks unsalted butter,
   at room temperature
250 g/1^1/$_4$ cups caster/superfine sugar
4 large eggs, beaten
1 teaspoon pure vanilla extract
250 g/2 cups plain/all-purpose flour
2 teaspoons baking powder
3–4 tablespoons milk,
   at room temperature

MEDIUM

175 g/1^1/$_2$ sticks unsalted butter,
   at room temperature
175 g/^{3}/$_4$ cup plus 2 tablespoons
   caster/superfine sugar
3 large eggs, beaten
1 teaspoon pure vanilla extract
175 g/1^1/$_3$ cups plain/all-purpose flour
1^1/$_2$ teaspoons baking powder
3 tablespoons milk,
   at room temperature

SMALL

125g/9 tablespoons unsalted butter,
   at room temperature
125 g/^{2}/$_3$ cup caster/superfine sugar
2 large eggs, beaten
^{1}/$_2$ teaspoon pure vanilla extract
125 g/1 cup plain/all-purpose flour
1 teaspoons baking powder
2 tablespoons milk,
   at room temperature

Preheat the oven to 180°C (350°F) Gas 4.

Cream the butter and sugar in an electric freestanding mixer or with a hand-held electric whisk until pale, light and fluffy, about 2–3 minutes. Very gradually add the beaten eggs, mixing well between each addition and scraping down the bowl with a rubber spatula from time to time. Stir in the vanilla extract.

Sift together the flour and baking powder and add to the cake mixture in two batches, mixing until smooth. Add the milk and mix until smooth.

Revert to the relevant cake recipe and continue as instructed.

ALTERNATIVE FLAVOURS

Basic Chocolate: substitute 4 tablespoons unsweetened cocoa powder for the same quantity of flour in the Extra Large mixture, 3 tablespoons in the Large, 2 in the Medium and 1 in the Small.

Lemon or Orange: substitute the grated zest of an unwaxed lemon or orange for the vanilla extract.

VANILLA CAKE

This makes for another great base but has a few tweaks compared to the mixtures on the previous page. It is best to stick to the specified recipe for each animal cake but, on a rainy day, why not give both mixtures a go and try to taste the difference!

350 g/2^2/$_3$ cups plain/all-purpose flour
3 teaspoons baking powder
1 teaspoon bicarbonate of/baking soda
a pinch of salt
225 g/2 sticks unsalted butter, at room temperature
350 g/1^3/$_4$ cups caster/superfine sugar
4 large eggs
1 teaspoon vanilla extract
250 ml/1 cup buttermilk, room temperature
2 23-cm/9-inch or 3 20-cm/8-inch cake pans, greased and lined

Preheat the oven to 180°C (350°F) Gas 4.

Sift together the flour, baking powder, bicarbonate of/baking soda and salt.

Cream the butter and sugar in the bowl of an electric freestanding mixer until really pale and light – at least 3–4 minutes.

Lightly beat the eggs and vanilla together. Gradually add to the creamed butter in 4 or 5 additions, mixing well between each addition and scraping down the bowl from time to time with a rubber spatula.

Add the sifted dry ingredients to the bowl alternately with the buttermilk. Mix until smooth.

Now turn to the relevant recipe and continue with the instructions, or if you want to bake the cake, divide the mixture evenly between the prepared pans and spread level with a palette knife/metal spatula. Bake the cakes on the middle shelf of the preheated oven for about 25 minutes or until an inserted skewer comes out clean.

Cool for 3–4 minutes in the pans, then remove to cool completely on a wire rack.

BUTTERMILK CAKE

This base can be used for both small and large cakes but, with its higher buttermilk to flour ratio (compared to the Vanilla Cake, opposite), it is best suited to some of the cupcake recipes in this book. Paper cupcake cases can vary enormously in size, so it's safest to suggest filling the cases two-thirds full. This recipe makes 12–16 regular cupcakes depending on the cases used. Undecorated cupcakes can be frozen in plastic airtight boxes and defrosted for another time.

175 g/1^1/$_2$ sticks unsalted butter, at room temperature
200 g/1 cup caster/superfine sugar
2 whole eggs and 1 egg yolk, beaten
1 teaspoon vanilla extract
225 g/1^3/$_4$ cups plain/all-purpose flour
1 teaspoon baking powder
^{1}/$_2$ teaspoon bicarbonate of/baking soda
125 ml/^{1}/$_2$ cup buttermilk

MAKES 12–16 CUPCAKES

Cream together the butter and sugar until light and creamy. Gradually add the beaten eggs, mixing well between each addition and scraping down the side of the mixing bowl from time to time. Add the vanilla.

Sift together the flour, baking powder and bicarbonate of/baking soda and add to the mixture in alternate batches with the buttermilk. Mix until smooth, then turn to the relevant recipe.

VANILLA CUPCAKES

This is a simple cupcake mixture to make. Here it's flavoured with pure vanilla extract but you could just as easily use lemon or orange extract, rosewater or coffee essence, if you prefer.

175 g/1½ sticks unsalted butter, at room temperature
175/¾ cup plus 2 tablespoons caster/
   superfine sugar
3 eggs, beaten
1 teaspoon pure vanilla extract
175 g/1⅓ cups plain/all-purpose flour
2 teaspoons baking powder
½ teaspoon bicarbonate of/baking soda
a pinch of salt
3 tablespoons sour cream, at room temperature
12-hole muffin pan, lined with cupcake cases

MAKES 12

Preheat the oven to 180°C (350°F) Gas 4. Cream the butter and sugar until pale, light and fluffy – about 3 minutes in an electric freestanding mixer.

Gradually add the beaten eggs, mixing well and scraping down the side of the bowl between each addition. Add the vanilla and mix again. Sift the flour, baking powder, bicarbonate of/baking soda and salt into the bowl, add the sour cream and fold in using a rubber spatula or a large metal spoon.

Once the mixture is smooth, divide it evenly between the cupcake cases and bake on the middle shelf of the preheated oven for about 20 minutes or until the cakes are golden, well risen and an inserted skewer comes out clean.

Cool for 3–4 minutes in the pans, then remove to cool completely on a wire rack.

CHOCOLATE CUPCAKES

Here is a delicious and just-as-easy chocolate cupcake recipe.

40 g/$^1/_3$ cup unsweetened cocoa powder
100 ml/$^1/_3$ cup plus 1 tablespoon boiling water
150 g/1$^1/_4$ sticks butter, at room temperature
175 g/$^3/_4$ cup plus 2 tablespoons caster/superfine sugar
2 large eggs, beaten
1 teaspoon pure vanilla extract
150 g/1 cup plus 2 tablespoons plain/all-purpose flour
2 teaspoons baking powder
$^1/_2$ teaspoon bicarbonate of/baking soda
a pinch of salt
2 tablespoons sour cream, at room temperature
12-hole muffin pan, lined with cupcake cases

MAKES 12

Preheat the oven to 180°C (350°F) Gas 4. Tip the cocoa into a small, heatproof bowl, add the boiling water and whisk until smooth. Set aside to cool.

Cream the butter and sugar until light and fluffy – about 3 minutes in an electric freestanding mixer. Gradually add the beaten eggs, mixing well and scraping down the side of the bowl between each addition. Add the vanilla and cocoa mixture and mix again. Sift the flour, baking powder, bicarbonate of/baking soda and salt into the bowl, add the sour cream and fold in using a rubber spatula or a large metal spoon.

Once the mixture is smooth, divide it evenly between the cupcake cases and bake on the middle shelf of the preheated oven for about 20 minutes or until the cakes are well risen and an inserted skewer comes out clean.

Cool for 3–4 minutes in the pans, then remove to cool completely on a wire rack.

BASIC VANILLA COOKIE DOUGH

If you can resist tucking into these delicious cookies straight from the oven, they will keep undecorated for up to 3 days in an airtight box. Once they've been decorated, they should be eaten within 24 hours.

225 g/2 sticks unsalted butter, at room temperature
225 g/1 cup plus 2 tablespoons caster/superfine sugar
1 egg, beaten
1/2 teaspoon pure vanilla extract
a pinch of salt
450 g/3 1/2 cups plain/all-purpose flour, sifted,
    plus extra for dusting

**MAKES ABOUT
12 LARGE COOKIES**

Cream together the butter and sugar until light and creamy. Add the beaten egg, vanilla and salt and mix well.

Gradually add the flour and mix until incorporated. Bring together into a dough, then flatten into a disc. Wrap in clingfilm/ plastic wrap and chill for 2 hours.

Roll the dough out on a lightly floured work surface to a thickness of 3–4 mm/1/8 inch, then turn to the relevant recipe.

Remember that once you have stamped out the shapes required in the individual recipes, you can gather the remaining dough together into a ball and re-roll to make more shapes. The shapes will then need to be chilled for a further 15 minutes before baking.

BASIC SPICED GINGERBREAD

Here is a simple, spiced gingerbread dough suitable for all the decorated cookies in this book. The recipe makes approximately 12 medium-sized cookies depending on the cutters used. If you like, add 1 tablespoon finely chopped crystallized ginger or candied peel to the dough to make the gingerbread more sophisticated.

2 tablespoons golden/light corn syrup
1 large egg yolk
200 g/1^2/$_3$ cups plain/all-purpose flour,
   plus extra for dusting
^{1}/$_2$ teaspoon baking powder
1^1/$_2$ teaspoons ground ginger
1 teaspoon ground cinnamon
^{1}/$_4$ teaspoon freshly grated nutmeg
a pinch of salt
100 g/7 tablespoons unsalted butter, chilled and diced
75 g/1^1/$_3$ cup light muscovado or light brown (soft) sugar

Beat together the golden/light corn syrup and egg yolk in a small bowl.

Sift the flour, baking powder, spices and salt into a food processor (or into a mixing bowl) and add the butter. Use the pulse button to process the mixture (or rub the butter into the flour mixture with your fingertips). When the mixture starts to look like sand and there are no lumps of butter, add the sugar and pulse (or mix with your fingers) again for 30 seconds to incorporate. With the motor running, add the egg-yolk mixture and pulse (or mix with a wooden spoon) until starting to clump together.

Tip the mixture out onto a very lightly floured surface and knead gently to bring together into a smooth ball. Flatten the dough into a disc, wrap in clingfilm/plastic wrap and chill for 1–2 hours. Now go to Step 4 of the chocolate gingerbread recipe opposite.

BASIC CHOCOLATE GINGERBREAD

This is a darker gingerbread dough with a hint of cocoa and a light smokiness from the treacle and dark brown sugar. The recipe will make approximately 12 cookies depending on the cutters used.

2 tablespoons golden/light corn syrup
2 tablespoons black treacle/molasses
1 large egg yolk
200 g/1^2/$_3$ cups plain/all-purpose flour,
   plus extra for dusting
1 teaspoon baking powder
25 g/3 tablespoons unsweetened cocoa powder
2 teaspoons ground ginger
^{1}/$_2$ teaspoon ground cinnamon
^{1}/$_4$ teaspoon freshly grated nutmeg
a pinch of salt
75 g/5 tablespoons unsalted butter, chilled and diced
75 g/1^1/$_3$ cup dark brown (soft) sugar
50 g/1^1/$_2$ cup ground almonds

Beat together the golden/light corn syrup, treacle/molasses and egg yolk in a small bowl.

Sift the flour, baking powder, cocoa, spices and salt into a food processor (or into a mixing bowl) and add the butter. When the mixture starts to look like sand and there are no lumps of butter, add the sugar and almonds and pulse (or mix with your fingers) again for 30 seconds to incorporate. With the motor running, add the egg yolk mixture and pulse (or mix with a wooden spoon) until starting to clump together.

Tip the mixture out onto a very lightly floured surface and knead gently to bring together into a smooth ball. Flatten the dough into a disc, wrap in clingfilm/plastic wrap and chill for 1–2 hours.

Preheat the oven to 170°C (325°F) Gas 3.

Lightly dust a clean, dry surface with flour and roll the dough evenly to a thickness of 2–3 mm/^{1}/$_8$ inch. Use a cutter or template to stamp out as many cookies as possible from the dough, cutting each one as close as possible to the next one. Arrange the cookies on baking sheets lined with baking parchment.

Gather the dough scraps together, knead lightly, re-roll and stamp out more cookies until all the dough has been used up.

Bake the gingerbread in batches on the middle shelf of the preheated oven. Keep an eye on the cookies, as you want them to brown evenly. You may have to turn the baking sheets around if your oven is hotter on one side than the other.

Allow the cookies to cool completely on the baking sheets before icing. Store undecorated gingerbread cookies in an airtight container for up to three days.

GINGERBREAD COOKIES

These cookies use more spices and have a little more 'kick' to them compared to the Basic Spiced Gingerbread recipe on the previous page. They will keep undecorated for three days in an airtight box. If they've been decorated, they should be eaten within 24 hours.

375 g/2¾ cups plus 1½ tablespoons plain/all-purpose flour
½ teaspoon baking powder
1 teaspoon bicarbonate of/baking soda
1 teaspoon ground cinnamon
3 teaspoons ground ginger
¼ teaspoon ground cloves
¼ teaspoon ground nutmeg
¼ teaspoon ground allspice
a pinch of cayenne pepper
a pinch of salt
125 g/9 tablespoons unsalted butter, at room temperature
75 g/⅓ cup light brown (soft) sugar
1 egg, beaten
50 ml/3½ tablespoons clear honey
50 ml/3½ black treacle/molasses
1 tablespoon freshly squeezed lemon juice

Sift together the flour, baking powder, bicarbonate of/baking soda, spices and salt.

Cream together the butter and sugar until light and creamy. Add the beaten egg, honey, treacle/molasses and lemon juice and mix until smooth. Add the sifted dry ingredients and mix again until smooth. Knead the dough lightly, just enough to bring it together, then wrap in clingfilm/plastic wrap and chill for 2 hours.

Now return to your specified recipe and follow the rest of the method.

VANILLA BUTTERCREAM

Buttercream is a dream to pipe and the easiest coating for cakes of any shape.

350 g/3 sticks unsalted butter, at room temperature
700 g/5 cups icing/confectioners' sugar, sifted
pure vanilla extract (optional)

Cream the butter in an electric freestanding mixer or in a large bowl with a hand-held electric whisk until really soft. Gradually beat in the icing/confectioners' sugar until pale and smooth. Add a few drops of vanilla extract, if using.

MERINGUE BUTTERCREAM

This is a great frosting. For a buttercream it's surprisingly light due to the addition of meringue. It's versatile and can be flavoured with chocolate (see final step) vanilla, lemon or coffee extract, or even strawberry jam/jelly and lemon curd. It's important to add the butter only once the meringue is cooled otherwise it will melt and make the frosting curdle.

275 g/1½ cups minus 2 tablespoons caster/
   superfine sugar
4 large egg whites
a pinch of salt
350 g/3 sticks unsalted butter, at room temperature
   and diced
1 teaspoon pure vanilla extract or the seeds from
   ½ vanilla pod/bean
sugar thermometer

Put the sugar, egg whites and salt in a medium heatproof bowl set over a pan of simmering water. Whisk slowly with a balloon whisk until the sugar has completely dissolved and the mixture is foamy. Continue to cook and whisk until the mixture reaches 60°C/140°F on a sugar thermometer – about 4 minutes.

Quickly pour the mixture into the bowl of an electric freestanding mixer and whisk on medium–high speed for 3 minutes, or until cooled, thick, stiff and glossy. Gradually add the butter, beating constantly, until the frosting is smooth. Fold in the vanilla and use immediately.

To make chocolate meringue buttercream, melt 150 g/5 oz. chopped dark/bittersweet chocolate, then leave to cool slightly. Stir into the buttercream at the same time as the vanilla.

MERINGUE FROSTING

When using this frosting, it helps to freeze the cake for 1 hour before icing. This makes the surface of the cake firmer and crumbs are less likely to spoil the clean, white finish of the frosting. Once the frosting has been cooked, work quickly to cover the cake using a palette knife/metal spatula dipped in hot water to make spreading easier.

250 g/1¼ cups caster/superfine sugar
4 large egg whites
a pinch of salt

Set a medium-large heatproof bowl over a pan of barely simmering water (do not let the base of the bowl touch the water). Put the sugar, egg whites, salt and 2 tablespoons water into the bowl and, using a hand-held electric whisk, whisk on medium speed so that the sugar completely dissolves into the egg whites. Continue to whisk until the meringue is white, soft and pillowy. Increase the speed to high and whisk for another minute until the meringue is hot, stiff and glossy.

Remove from the heat and continue whisking for a further minute until the meringue has cooled slightly. Working very quickly and using a palette knife/metal spatula dipped in hot water, spread the frosting over the cake.

CHOCOLATE FUDGE FROSTING

This frosting is so good, you'll be tempted to eat it straight from the bowl!

350 g/12 oz. dark/bittersweet chocolate, roughly chopped
225 g/2 sticks unsalted butter
225 ml/scant 1 cup full-fat/whole milk
1 teaspoon vanilla extract
450 g/3¼ cups icing/confectioners' sugar, sifted

Melt the chocolate and butter together in a heatproof bowl set over a pan of barely simmering water (do not let the base of the bowl touch the water). Stir until melted and smooth, then set aside to cool slightly.

In another bowl, whisk together the milk, vanilla extract and icing/confectioners' sugar until smooth. Add the cooled chocolate mixture and stir until smooth. Leave the frosting to set and thicken up slightly before use.

ROYAL ICING

500 g/1 lb. 2 oz. royal icing sugar/mix
75–100 ml/about ⅓ cup cold water
OR
500 g/3½ cups icing/confectioners' sugar
2 large egg whites

USING ROYAL ICING/SUGAR MIX

Tip the royal icing sugar/mix into a large mixing
bowl and add the water gradually, mixing with a
whisk or wooden spoon until the icing is smooth and
thick enough that it will hold a ribbon trail when the
spoon or whisk is lifted from the bowl. This will be the
consistency that you need for piping outlines or details
on the cookies. You may need to add slightly more
or less water to achieve the right balance.

USING ICING/CONFECTIONERS' SUGAR

Note: This method uses raw eggs. Follow the method
above, but use the egg whites in place of the water.

TINTING ICING

Divide the icing into separate bowls. It is
best to use gel or paste food colouring
for tinting royal icing. This is available
in small pots and in a vast array of
colours. A small amount of colouring
goes a long way, so use it with
caution. Using a cocktail stick/
toothpick, gradually add dots
of colouring to the icing and
mix well before adding more
colour until you achieve the
desired shade.

PREPARING FOR FLOOD ICING

Fill the appropriate number of pastry/piping bags
with enough icing to pipe any outlines or details. The
remaining icing will be used for flooding the outlines
and will need to be slightly runnier, so add a drop more
water to make it more like the consistency of double/
heavy cream. Keep your icing covered when you're
not using it to prevent it from drying out. You will need
pastry/piping bags to create the outlines and details
on each cookie. Clear plastic disposable bags are
the best thing for this purpose, or make your own
(see page 29). They are readily available from good
kitchenware shops, sugarcraft specialists and online
suppliers and often come in packs of 24.

FLOODING TECHNIQUE

Spoon the icing into the pastry/piping bag, squeeze
the icing towards the tip and twist the top to prevent
any icing leaking out. Using sharp scissors, snip a tiny
point off the end of the bag.

Carefully pipe a fine outline around the edge of each
cookie in the shape that you require. Leave this to dry
for at least 10 minutes before flooding the middle with
the runnier icing. You can either do this with the pastry/
piping bag again, or with a teaspoon or a tiny spatula.
Make sure the icing evenly fills the outline. Keep the
filled icing bags wrapped in clingfilm/plastic wrap
when not in use so that the icing doesn't dry out.

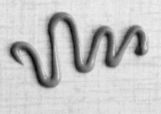

DECORATION TERMS & TIPS

**FLOWER MODELLING PASTE/
SUGAR FLORIST PASTE**

Flower modelling paste/sugar florist paste is
ideal for modelling and cutting into decorative
shapes. It is available ready-to-use – simply follow
the manufacturer's instructions. It can be found
in white in many supermarkets, but for a wider
range of colours, go to a specialist shop.

SUGAR PASTE/FONDANT ICING

Fondant icing is also readily available and sold in
blocks. It requires rolling out on a work surface that
has been lightly dusted with icing/confectioners' sugar.
Use gel or paste food colouring to tint the icing to your
desired shade. Once iced, cover the cake and leave
it for at least 4 hours to allow the icing to dry.

READY-ROLLED ICING

Ready-rolled sugar paste/fondant icing can easily
be found in most supermarkets' home baking sections
and usually come in a circle ready for icing a round
cake. It is best to cover the cake first in a thin layer
of either buttercream or marzipan.

WRITING ICING

Ready-to-use writing icing tubes are widely available
in the baking sections of most supermarkets and come
in a selection of colours but mainly red, green, black
and yellow. They are ideal when small amounts of icing
are required for writing letters, numbers and words on
cakes and for drawing outlines. They are small and
easy for children to use without getting too messy!
Look out for gel and sparkly writing icing, too.

TINTING WITH FOOD COLOURING

Gel or paste food colouring tend to be stronger than
liquid colours and come in a vast selection of colours.
They can be used to tint sugar paste/fondant icing and
buttercream, and are generally available from cake
decorating supply shops and online suppliers. A small
amount gives a good colour without watering down
the icing. Gradually add the paste using the point
of a cocktail stick/toothpick or wooden skewer and
mix well or knead into the icing until you have the
shade you're after.

SPRINKLES AND SWEETS/CANDIES

Most supermarkets carry a wide range of edible
decorating sprinkles in the home baking section, ranging
from multicoloured sprinkles to edible silver sugar pearls
and shapes especially for Halloween and Christmas.
Specialist cake decorating shops generally stock a
wide range of sprinkles in many shapes and colours.
Sweet/candy shops are a fantastic source for cake
decorations – liquorice shapes, chocolate
buttons, candy-coated chocolate drops
and marshmallows can all be used
to great effect on cakes.

MAKING SHAPES WITH SUGAR PASTE

When making flowers or other shapes to decorate a cake, flower modelling paste/sugar florist paste is the best thing to use. It generally comes in small packs and usually in white or ivory, although it is also available in a range of colours at specialist sugercraft suppliers online. It is, however, easy to tint whichever shade you like, using gel or paste food colouring.

Break off a small amount of paste at a time and keep the remainder tightly covered with clingfilm/plastic wrap to prevent it from drying out. Very lightly dust the work surface with icing/confectioners' sugar or rub a little groundnut or sunflower oil onto the area on which you are working. Using a small rolling pin, roll out the sugar paste as thinly as possible – roughly 1 mm/$\frac{1}{32}$ inch thick – and stamp out shapes or petals using cutters. Use your fingers to bend and shape the leaves or petals and then let dry on a tray or baking sheet covered with baking parchment. Repeat with the remaining sugar paste. See page 114 for some beautiful sugar-paste butterflies and flowers.

Decorate sugar-paste shapes with finely piped dots of tinted royal icing left plain or adorned with sprinkles/nonpareils. If you can't get hold of flower modelling paste/sugar florist paste, you can use sugar paste/fondant icing, however it lacks the delicacy of flower modelling paste/sugar florist paste and is not as easy to use. You will also find that it will not roll out as thinly and it takes longer to dry.

SUGAR-PASTE DAISIES

Tint some flower modelling paste/sugar florist paste your chosen colour by gradually adding gel or paste food colouring and kneading it in until completely incorporated. Very lightly dust the work surface with icing/confectioners' sugar and roll out some sugar paste to a thickness of about 1 mm/$\frac{1}{32}$ inch.

Using daisy cutters in assorted sizes, stamp out shapes from the sugar paste and leave to dry on scrunched up baking parchment – this will give the flowers a shapely curl. Scoop 2 tablespoons of pre-made royal icing into a small bowl and tint yellow using gel or paste food colouring. Spoon this into a pastry/piping bag (see pages 28–9) and pipe a yellow dot into the middle of each daisy. Leave to dry for at least 24 hours.

CRUMB COATING

A spoonful of icing spread onto the middle of your cake board will stop your cake from moving around. When crumb-coating it's best to apply the buttercream little and often, this will help to give an even distribution and prevent dragging crumbs around the cake. Use the tip of a dinner knife to apply icing to the sides and top of your stacked cake, slightly spreading a little more buttercream into any gaps or recesses, if necessary.

Smooth the top with a palette knife/metal spatula. At this stage, the sides do not need to be completely smooth. When the cake is covered, take the palette knife/metal spatula or a cake scraper and hold vertically at a 45° angle against the cake. Sweep around the cake with a little pressure to remove the excess icing. Scrape this icing into a separate bowl (as it may have crumbs in) and continue to remove the excess buttercream. If there are any gaps or holes, fill with a little buttercream and smooth again with the palette knife/metal spatula or cake scraper.

After finishing the sides, you will have little peaks at the top edge of your cake. Use the palette knife/metal spatula, held horizontally, to draw these peaks into the centre of the cake, using gentle but sturdy sweeping motions. Chill the cake for 15 minutes.

PIPING NOZZLES/
TIPS AND BAGS

If you plan on making lots of decorated cakes and cookies, it is worth considering investing in a selection of piping nozzles/tips in varying shapes and sizes. Pastry/piping bags also come in a variety of materials and sizes. Look out for easy-to-use disposable plastic pastry/piping bags that usually come in packs of 24 and can be trimmed either to a point or to fit most piping nozzles/tips, or make your own as described opposite.

(1)

(2)

(3)

(4)

HOW TO MAKE 2 PAPER PASTRY/PIPING BAGS

• Cut a large piece baking parchment into a square. Fold the square in half diagonally, then cut along the fold to give you 2 triangles.

• Take 1 triangle. With the longest side closest to you, take the right-hand corner and turn it inwards towards the top corner to create the start of a cone. (1)

• Wrap the left-hand corner around the cone. (2)

• The left-hand corner should meet the top of the cone, underneath and facing the original, right-hand corner. Neaten the points so that you have a tight cone. (3)

• Flatten the cone – there will now be a triangle of paper sticking out of the top. Fold this over a few times to secure the bag. (4)

• Snip off the pointed end – this will be the nozzle/tip. (5)

• Repeat to make another pastry/piping bag.

(5)

Fantastical
CREATURES

ULTIMATE UNICORN

1 quantity Extra Large Basic Vanilla
Cake mixture (see page 11)
2 quantities Vanilla Buttercream
(see page 20, but made with
white vegetable fat, such as Trex
or Cookeen, instead of butter)
pink, orange, yellow, green,
blue and purple gel or paste
food colouring

TO DECORATE
220 g/8 oz. white flower
modelling paste
edible glue (optional)
gold edible spray
gold edible lustre
icing/confectioners' sugar,
for dusting
15 g/$^1/_2$ oz. black fondant icing
black writing icing pen
white sugar pearls
wooden skewer
7-cm/2$^3/_4$-inch round
pastry/cookie cutter
5.5-cm/2$^1/_4$-inch round
pastry/cookie cutter
3-cm/1$^1/_4$-inch round
pastry/cookie cutter
3 pastry/piping bags, each fitted
with a different large star
nozzle/tip, or make your own
(see page 29)
3 x 18-cm/7-inch cake pans,
greased and lined with
baking parchment

Serves 20

Start with the horn. Divide 120 g/4 oz. white modelling paste in two and roll each into a pointed sausage shape. Brush one with a line of water then place the other on top. Twist together, gently holding the tips, then trim the base flat so the horn is 13 cm/5$^1/_4$ inches long. Brush the gaps with edible glue or water. Brush the end of a skewer with water and insert into the base about halfway up. Leave to set overnight. Spray with edible gold, allow to dry, then brush with gold lustre.

For the ears, halve the remaining modelling paste and tint one half pale pink. Dust a surface with icing/confectioners' sugar and roll out both pastes to 2 mm/$^1/_{16}$ inch thick. Use the largest cutter to cut out two circles of white. Use the medium-sized cutter to cut out two circles of pink, then cut into 'leaf' shapes. Brush one side of each pink shape with water and stick to the circles. Pinch together the two ends of each ear. Leave to set overnight.

Preheat the oven to 180°C (350°F) Gas 4. Divide the cake mixture between six bowls. Stir a different food colouring into each bowl, until each is a mid-tone. Transfer three mixtures to the prepared pans, and cover the remaining bowls with clingfilm/plastic wrap. Bake for 15–20 minutes until an inserted skewer comes out clean. Cool for 10 minutes in the pans, then remove to cool completely on a wire rack. Wash the pans and grease and line again. Transfer the three remaining mixtures and bake as above.

If necessary, trim the tops of the cakes to make them level. Sandwich together using 600 g/1lb 5 oz. buttercream – the bottom side of the top cake should be facing up. Crumb-coat (see page 27) the cake using 450 g/1 lb buttercream. Chill for 15 minutes. Coat the cake in a second layer using 450 g/1 lb of the remaining buttercream. Smooth and remove the excess with a palette knife/metal spatula. Insert the unicorn horn into a central position.

For the eyes, dust a surface with icing/confectioners' sugar and roll out the black fondant icing to 2 mm/$^1/_{16}$ inch thick. Use the smallest round cutter to create to slim crescent shapes and stick these onto position on your cake, using the writing icing pen to draw on eyelashes.

Divide the remaining buttercream between four bowls. Tint one bowl pink, one yellow, one blue and one green. Fill the pastry/piping bags, spreading at least two colours in each side of the bags to create the rainbow mane. Start with a rose shape at the front of the cake, then – using alternate star-shaped nozzles/tips – work from the top of the cake and down one side, so you can still see the mane from the front of the cake. Gently insert the ears either side but slightly further back from the horn. Scatter over a few sugar pearls.

Grab your magic whisk and 'wow' guests by conjuring up this classic unicorn cake. Once you've mastered tinting each layer in the suggested shades, why not try different combinations for this creation that's as pretty as a rainbow on the inside and out!

FIERY PHOENIX

1 quantity **Extra Large Basic
Chocolate Cake mixture (see
page 11) baked in three 18-cm/
7-inch greased and lined cake
pans for 35–40 minutes, until
an inserted skewer comes out
clean, then cooled**

1/3 quantity **Vanilla Buttercream
(see page 20)**

1 quantity **Chocolate Fudge Frosting
(see page 21 – leave to cool and
thicken at room temperature for
at least 4 hours, then colour with
black gel or paste food colouring
and stir through with a metal
spoon after standing)**

TO DECORATE

**50 g metalic gold flower
modelling paste**

**50 g/1³/4 oz. each red and
orange fondant icing**

**icing/confectioners' sugar,
for dusting**

**100 g/³/4 cup each red and orange
clear hard-boiled sweets/
hard candies**

*paper template of a phoenix about
10 x 15 cm/4 x 6 inches (draw
freehand and cut out with scissors
or search online for 2D phoenix
pictures to print and cut out)*

sugar paste knife tool

pastry/piping bag

mini food processor/blender

4 small skewers

3–5 cocktail sticks/toothpicks

*2 large baking sheets, lined
with baking parchment*

Serves 20

First, trim the tops of the cakes to make level, if necessary. Sandwich together using the buttercream – the bottom side of the top cake should be facing up. Place the cake on a serving plate or cake board.

Reserve 200 g/7 oz. chocolate fudge frosting. Crumb-coat (see page 27) the cake using 300 g/10¹/2 oz. chocolate fudge frosting. Smooth and remove the excess frosting with a palette knife/ metal spatula. Chill for 20 minutes. Use the remaining frosting to repeat as above with a second layer.

To make the phoenix, knead the gold modelling paste until soft. Roll out on a sheet of baking parchment to 2 mm/¹/16 inch thick, dusting the rolling pin with icing/confectioners' sugar, if necessary. Place your template on top and cut around the outline using the sugar paste knife tool (reserve the trimmings). Gently press the phoenix to the front of the cake.

Roll out the red and orange fondant icing and re-roll the reserved gold modelling paste trimmings on baking parchment each to 2 mm/¹/16 inch. Using the sugar paste knife tool, cut out ten large red flame-shapes by freehand, to various heights. Then cut out ten slightly smaller orange flame-shapes and finally ten small gold flame-shapes. Stick one on top of the other so you can see all three colours on each, brushing one side of the orange and gold shapes with a little water to help stick, if necessary. Stick the flames all around the side of the cake.

Fill the pastry/piping bag with the reserved frosting. Snip 1.5 cm/⁵/8 inch at the tip of the bag and pipe small blobs around the top of the cake.

For the top flames, in a mini food processor/blender, process each of the hard-boiled sweets/hard candies separately to a sugar-like consistency. Lay the skewers and cocktail sticks/toothpicks onto the baking sheet lined with parchment, keeping them well spaced apart. Put the orange sugar in a very small saucepan and gently heat until melted. Shake the pan towards the end to allow any unmelted sugar to melt. Using the same technique, melt the red sugar at the same time in a separate pan.

Working fairly quickly, drizzle the orange liquid over the tips of the skewers and cocktail sticks/toothpicks. Drizzle a few blobs directly onto the parchment, drawing slightly crossways at the tip to create a flame-shape. Before it sets spoon the red liquid into the base of each 'flame' to enhance the fire-effect. Allow to set. Insert the flames on skewers and cocktail sticks/toothpicks into the centre of the cake and gently sit the flames without sticks onto the top of cake.

CHINESE DRAGON

1 quantity Large Basic Vanilla or
Chocolate Cake mixture (see
page 11) baked in two 23-cm/
9-inch greased and lined cake
pans for 35–40 minutes, until
an inserted skewer comes out
clean, then cooled
1 quantity Vanilla Buttercream
(see page 20)

TO DECORATE
red and orange gel or paste food
colouring
15 g/$\frac{1}{2}$ oz. red fondant icing
2 chocolate drops
2 Polo/round breath mints
3–4 red liquorice strips/shoelaces
1 orange and 1 yellow jelly
snake, cut in half widthways,
then cut in half lengthways
2 orange Smarties/candy-coated
chocolates
12 jelly diamonds
4 thin square mint-filled chocolates,
such as After Eights
*cake board, at least 33 x 43cm/
13 x 17 inches*
*2.5-cm/1-inch round
pastry/cookie cutter*
**For the wings you will also need
(optional)**
*2 x 8-cm/3-inch squares of thin
orange card*
Sellotape
2 cocktail sticks/toothpicks
glue

Serves 20

To start, cut one of the cakes in half to create two semi-circles. Sandwich the tops together with 100 g/3$\frac{1}{2}$ oz. buttercream. Place 'straight-side-down' in the centre of the cake board and secure in place with a little buttercream. Cut the second cake in half to make two further semi-circles. Cut one semi circle in half lengthways and cross ways – the two curved pieces will make the back legs, the more-rectangular pieces will make the head and neck. Face the remaining semi circle curved edge towards you. Working from the left, measure 5 cm/2 inches in from the straight top and cut a half-crescent shape, tapering to a point at the top of the right side of the semi-circle. This will be the tail. Trim the remaining piece of cake along the curve to make it an even semi-circle, then cut it in half crossways to make the two front legs.

Use 100 g/3$\frac{1}{2}$ oz. buttercream to stick the pieces together; on one side of the back legs spread buttercream and attach to the main body. Repeat with the front legs. Position and secure the tail in place. Position one of the remaining pieces in front of the 'body' to make the neck, trim vertically (reserve the trimming) then position the final piece at a right angle to create the head. Secure the pieces in place with buttercream. Carve the reserved piece into a dome and secure in place with buttercream on top of the head to make a rounded face. Shave the corners from the end of the snout.

Put 200 g/7 oz. of the buttercream in a bowl and tint it red. Tint the remaining buttercream orange. Reserve 200 g/7 oz. of the orange and use the rest to coat the cake in a thin layer. Chill for 20 minutes. Coat the cake in a second layer – apply orange on the legs and lower half and red on the top. Blend the colours a little, then smooth with a palette knife/metal spatula.

Roll 10 g/$\frac{1}{3}$ oz. of the red fondant icing into two balls. Flatten slightly and press into each of them with the end of wooden spoon to make a small indentation. Put into position on the buttercream 'snout' for nostrils.

For the eyes, place a chocolate drop into each mint hole. Put into position. Roll out the remaining red fondant as thin as possible on baking parchment. Use the cutter to cut out a circle and cut in half to drape over the eyes for lids. Mark a mouth-shape with a knife and insert the liquorice and jelly snakes to create fire. Place the Smarties/candy-coated chocolates on the top of the head for ears. Put the jelly diamonds at the bottom of the legs for claws. Cut four mint-filled chocolates diagonally for spikes along the top of the dragon.

If making wings, fold the card pieces in half diagonally. Sellotape a cocktail stick/toothpick along the fold then glue the sides of the card together. Cut a wavy pattern along two edges of each wing. Insert into the top of the body.

WISE OWL

Usually known as a loyal companion to magical witches and wizards, this wise owl would fit in at spooky- or magic-themed parties. To decorate, look out for chocolate buttons in all different sizes.

1 quantity Extra Large Basic
  Vanilla or Chocolate Cake
  mixture (see page 11)
1 quantity Chocolate Fudge
  Frosting (see page 21)

TO DECORATE
chocolate buttons in different sizes
chocolate sprinkles
1 flaked chocolate bar
1 chocolate-covered toffee bar
*2 x 23-cm/9-inch cake pans,
  greased and lined with
  baking parchment*
*pastry/piping bag, fitted with
  a star-shaped nozzle/tip, or
  make your own (see page 29)*

Serves 12–16

Preheat the oven to 180°C (350°F) Gas 4.

Make the vanilla or chocolate cake mixture and divide between the prepared cake pans. Bake on the middle shelf of the preheated oven for 30–35 minutes until an inserted skewer comes out clean. Cool for 10 minutes in the pans, then remove to cool completely on a wire rack.

Level off the tops of the cakes with a sharp knife, if necessary. Place one cake on a serving plate and spread the cut surface with about 3 tablespoons of the chocolate fudge frosting. Cover with the other cake layer, cut-side down. Coat the top and sides of the whole cake with three-quarters of the remaining frosting, spreading evenly with a palette knife/metal spatula.

Arrange the chocolate buttons over the bottom half of the cake to resemble feathers and cover the top half of the cake with chocolate sprinkles. Fill the pastry/piping bag with the remaining frosting and use this to pipe feathers around the owl's face.

Position assorted chocolate buttons on top of the sprinkles for the eyes. Cut the flaked chocolate bar into thin pieces and push into the bottom edge of the cake to make legs. Cut the toffee bar in half. Slice one half diagonally into two pieces for the wings and push one into each side of the owl. Cut the remaining piece of toffee bar at an angle to make a beak and position on the owl's face.

JOLLY GREEN DINOSAUR

This is guaranteed to appeal to the dinosaur-loving birthday boy or girl. Look out for chocolate-coated wafers in the cookie aisle of the supermarket as they make ideal spines. Decorate the serving plate with chocolate-coated 'boulders'.

1 quantity Extra Large Basic Vanilla Cake mixture (see page 11)
1 quantity Vanilla Buttercream (see page 20)

TO DECORATE
green and brown gel or paste food colouring
14 mini chocolate drops
chocolate-coated wafers
green diamond-shaped sweets/candies
chocolate sprinkles
green sprinkles
2 white chocolate buttons
black writing icing
2 x 23-cm/9-inch cake pans, greased and lined with baking parchment
pastry/piping bag, fitted with a star-shaped nozzle/tip, or make your own (see page 29)

Serves 10–12

Preheat the oven to 180°C (350°F) Gas 4.

Make the vanilla cake mixture and divide between the prepared cake pans. Bake on the middle shelf of the preheated oven for 35–40 minutes until an inserted skewer comes out clean. Cool for 10 minutes in the pans, then remove to cool completely on a wire rack. Store overnight in an airtight container.

The next day, assemble the dinosaur. Use a long, serrated knife to level the tops of the cakes, if necessary. Lay the cakes one on top of the other, cut sides facing each other. Cut the bottom third off both cakes and reserve. Separate the cakes again and spread some of the buttercream over one cut side. Sandwich the 2 cakes together, then place upright (resting on the flat side) in the middle of a serving plate.

The reserved pieces of cake should look like orange segments. Take one segment and cut it in half to make two rough triangle shapes. Sandwich the two shapes together with a little buttercream and position upright as the head of the dinosaur. Cut two strips from the straight side of the remaining segment and stick 2 strips with buttercream on each side of the dinosaur to make each leg. You should have a slim segment shape leftover. Cut this in half to make two rough triangle shapes. Sandwich the two shapes together with a little buttercream and position upright as the tail.

Reserve 4 tablespoons of the buttercream in a small bowl. Tint the remaining buttercream green with the green food colouring. Fill the pastry/piping bag with the green buttercream and use to cover the dinosaur with rosettes. Tint the reserved buttercream brown and pipe little feet onto the legs. Press on the mini chocolate buttons for the claws, three on each foot.

Push the chocolate-coated wafers all down the back of the dinosaur to make scales and position the green jelly diamonds in between each wafer. Scatter the chocolate and green sprinkles all over the dinosaur. Stick the white chocolate drops on the face for the eyes and use the black writing icing for the centre of the eyes and to make a mouth. Position the last mini chocolate drops as nostrils.

BUBBLY NARWHAL

1 quantity Extra Large Basic Vanilla
  Cake mixture (see page 11) baked
  in three 18-cm/7-inch greased
  and lined cake pans for 35–40
  minutes, until an inserted skewer
  comes out clean, then cooled
1½ quantities Vanilla Buttercream
  (see page 20)

TO DECORATE
15 g/½ oz. white flower
  modelling paste
edible silver lustre
150 g/5½ oz. blue flower
  modelling paste
2 black sugar pearls
blue gel or paste food colouring
60 g/2 oz. multicoloured sprinkles
1 large egg white
125 g/4½ oz. icing/confectioners'
  sugar, plus extra for dusting
¼ teaspoon glycerine (optional –
  this will prevent the 'drips' from
  setting quite so hard but it will
  still work without)
1 teaspoon white sugar pearls
7–10 mint imperials
2 cocktail sticks/toothpicks,
  cut in half
thin paintbrush
3-cm/1¼-inch round
  pastry/cookie cutter

Serves 30

Start with the horn. Take 10 g/⅓ oz. white modelling paste, divide in two and roll each into a pointed sausage shape. Brush one with a line of water and place the other on top. Twist together, gently holding the tips, trim the base and brush the gaps with water. Brush the pointy end of one of the cocktail stick/toothpick halves with water and insert into the horn base, leaving 1 cm/⅜ inch visible. Leave to set for 4 hours. Brush with the silver lustre.

For the fins, take 15 g/½ oz. blue modelling paste. Dust a surface with icing/confectioners' sugar and roll it to 2 mm/1/16 inch thick. Use the cutter to stamp out a circle. Cut in half to make semi-circles and drape over a wooden spoon handle to create a wave shape in the middle. Leave to set for 4 hours.

For the body, roll the remaining blue modelling paste into a rounded cone, flatten the pointed end, then cut out a triangle to make the tail. Drape the tail over a small rolling pin. Keep in position while you add the eyes and mouth; roll two small, flattened balls using the white modelling paste. Brush one side of each with a little water and stick to each side of the head. Make two divots in each with a paintbrush end, brush with a little water, then push in the black sugar pearls. Use the paintbrush end to mark a smiley mouth into the face.

Brush the cut end of two cocktail sticks with water and push each into the lower half of the middle of the sides of the body (the fins will rest of these once they are dry). Brush the horn's cocktail stick/toothpick with a little water then insert into the top of the head. Set aside to dry overnight.

If necessary, trim the tops of the cakes to make level. Reserve 1 teaspoon buttercream. Tint 150 g/5½ oz. buttercream blue. Set both aside. Sandwich the cakes together using 300 g/10½ oz. plain buttercream – the bottom side of the top cake facing up. Place on a serving plate and crumb-coat (see page 27) using 400 g/14 oz. of the buttercream. Chill for 15 minutes. Coat in a second layer using the remaining buttercream. Smooth and remove excess with a palette knife/metal spatula. Smear blobs of blue buttercream around the cake and smooth. Press 50 g/1¾ oz. sprinkles around the bottom edge.

For the 'drips', whisk the egg white in a bowl until frothy. While whisking, add the sugar gradually, continuing until it holds soft peaks. If using, stir through the glycerine, and tint light blue. If needed, add a few drops of water to make a pouring texture. Pour over the cake, with drips down the sides. Level the top. Scatter over the remaining sprinkles, some white sugar pearls and a few mint imperials. Allow to set and place the narwhal on top, securing in place with buttercream. Put the fins in place. Add the remaining white sugar pearls and mint imperials to the side of the cake to create a bubble effect.

UNICORN CUPCAKES

These cupcakes will brighten up a table display at any kind of occasion –
from a baby shower to unicorn-themed birthday party!

1 quantity Vanilla Cupcake
    mixture (see page 14) baked
    in 12 cupcake cases in a muffin
    pan for 20–25 minutes, until
    an inserted skewer comes out
    clean, then cooled
$^2/_3$ quantity Vanilla Buttercream
    (see page 20)

TO DECORATE
75 g/2$^2/_3$ oz. metallic gold
    modelling paste
edible gold lustre
80 g/3 oz. white flower
    modelling paste
pink, yellow and turquoise blue gel
    or paste food colouring
icing/confectioners' sugar,
    for dusting
edible white or iridescent
    glitter dust
12 cocktail sticks/toothpicks
thin paintbrush
2.5-cm/1-inch round
    pastry/cookie cutter
3 medium and 1 large
    pastry/piping bags, or make
    your own (see page 29)
large star-shaped nozzle/tip

Makes 12

First, make the horns. Take two hazelnut-sized pieces of metallic gold modelling paste and roll each into a pointed sausage shape approximately 5 cm/2 inches long. Brush one with a line of water and place the other on top. Twist together, gently holding the tips, trim the base and brush the gaps with water. Brush the pointy end of a cocktail stick/toothpick in water and insert into the base of the horn about halfway up. Repeat until you have 12 horns. Leave to set for 1–2 hours. Brush with the gold lustre.

For the ears, halve the white modelling paste and tint one half pastel pink. Dust a surface with icing/confectioners' sugar and roll out the white and the pink flower modelling paste to 2 mm/$^1/_{16}$ inch thick. Use the cutter to stamp out 24 circles of the white modelling paste for the backs of the ears. Use the same cutter to stamp out 24 circles of the pink icing for the fronts of the ears, then cut into each of the pink circles to create smaller 'leaf' shapes. Discard the trimmings. Brush one side of each pink shape with water and stick to the circles. Pinch together the two ends of each ear. Leave to set for 1–2 hours.

Divide the buttercream between three bowls. Colour one bowl pastel pink, one lemon yellow and the final one pale turquoise blue.

Spoon each buttercream into separate medium-sized pastry/piping bags (without nozzles/tips), being careful not to overfill them. Snip the ends off each, leaving a 1–2-cm/$^1/_2$–$^3/_4$-inch hole. Snip the end off the large bag, fit it with the star nozzle/tip, then put the three filled medium-sized bags into it. Make sure the inner bags are pushed all the way down towards the nozzle/tip, then pipe onto your cupcakes for a three-tone effect.

Finish by topping the cupcakes with unicorn ears and horns (inserting the cocktail sticks/toothpicks into the baked cupcake). Dust with the edible white or iridescent glitter dust.

A PARLIAMENT OF OWLS

These wide-eyed creatures require no fancy cookie cutters – just round cutters in assorted sizes. These here are made into brown owls, but, if you're feeling creative, there's no reason why they couldn't be tawny or even snowy owls.

Basic Spiced Gingerbread (see page 18)
plain/all-purpose flour, for dusting
Royal Icing (see page 22)

TO DECORATE
yellow, black and brown gel or paste food colouring
assorted round cutters between 6 cm/2¹/₂ inches and 8 cm/3¹/₄ inches
baking sheets, lined with baking parchment
pastry/piping bags fitted with a fine writing nozzle/tip, or make your own (see page 29)

Makes 10–12

Prepare the basic spiced gingerbread, stopping at the end of Step 3. Preheat the oven to 160°C (325°F) Gas 3.

Lightly dust a clean, dry surface with flour and roll the dough evenly to a thickness of 3 mm/¹/₈ inch. Use the cutters to stamp out as many cookies as possible from the dough, cutting each one as close as possible to the next one. Arrange the cookies on the prepared baking sheets. Gather the dough scraps together, knead lightly, re-roll and stamp out more cookies until all the dough has been used up. Bake the gingerbread in batches on the middle shelf of the preheated oven for 10–12 minutes or until firm and lightly browned at the edges. Allow the cookies to cool completely on the baking sheets before icing.

Prepare the royal icing. Reserve 3 tablespoons in the mixing bowl, cover and set aside. Put 2 tablespoons in a small bowl and tint it yellow. Tint another 2 tablespoons black. Cover and set aside. Tint the remaining icing brown.

Fill the pastry/piping bag with 3 tablespoons of the brown icing and pipe the outline of an owl on each cookie. (See page 22 for instructions on flooding.) Allow to dry for at least 10 minutes.

Flood the insides of the outlines with brown icing. Allow to dry for 20 minutes.

Colour the remaining brown icing a deeper shade of brown, spoon into a pastry/piping bag and pipe fine feathers in swirly rows over the owls' bodies. Fill another pastry/piping bag with the reserved black icing and pipe 2 circles for the eyes. Allow to set, then flood with white icing. Using the tip of a knife, make a triangular beak and feet with the reserved yellow icing. Complete the eyes with black dots. Allow to dry completely before serving perched on tree branches.

A DAY AT THE *Zoo*

KING OF THE JUNGLE LION

Make a party roar with this little fella! If you're running low on black fondant icing, chocolate drops for eyes and nose, or liqourice strips for brows, work just as well.

1 quantity Large Basic Chocolate Cake mixture (see page 11) baked in two 23-cm/9-inch greased and lined round cake pans for 35–40 minutes, until an inserted skewer comes out clean, then cooled

1 quantity Vanilla Buttercream (see page 20)

TO DECORATE
yellow gel or paste food colouring
icing/confectioners' sugar, for dusting
100 g/3¹/₂ oz. white fondant icing
6 black sugar pearls
20 g/³/₄ oz. black fondant icing
2 white sugar pearls
100 g/3¹/₂ oz. yellow fondant icing
400 g/scant 1¹/₄ cups chocolate and hazelnut spread
6-cm/2¹/₂-inch round pastry/cookie cutter
3-cm/1¹/₄-inch round pastry/cookie cutter
2-cm/³/₄-inch round pastry/cookie cutter
thin paintbrush
pastry/piping bag, fitted with a grass-shaped nozzle/tip, or make your own (see page 29)
4 small wooden skewers

Serves 16

Start by assembling the cakes. If necessary, trim the tops of the cakes to make them level. Sandwich together using 200 g/7 oz. of the buttercream – the bottom side of the top cake should be facing up. Place on a serving plate and crumb-coat (see page 27) the cake using 300 g/10¹/₂ oz. of the buttercream. Chill for 15 minutes.

Place the remaining buttercream in a bowl and tint it yellow. Use to coat the cake in a second layer of buttercream. Smooth and remove the excess buttercream with a palette knife/metal spatula.

Dust a clean surface with icing/confectioners' sugar and roll out the white fondant icing to 3 mm/¹/₈ inch thick. Use the largest cutter to cut out three circles for the mouth detail. Stamp twice into the third circle to create the chin shape. Position on top of the cake leaving at least a 3-cm/1¹/₄-inch border around the edge. Use the medium-sized cutter to cut out two circles for the whites of the eyes. Position on top of the cake.

With the paintbrush end, make three indentations on each of the white cheeks. Brush with a dot of water and stick a black sugar pearl in each one.

Halve the black fondant icing and roll out on baking parchment to 2 mm/¹/₁₆ inch thick and use the medium-sized cutter to create eyebrow shapes – cut two circles, then use the cutter to cut into each one to create two crescent-shapes. Place on the cake at least 3 cm/1¹/₄ inches from the edge, then use the smallest cutter to cut out two circles for the pupils of the eyes. Brush one side of each with water and stick to the white circles. Make an indentation on each pupil with the paintbrush end. Brush with a dot of water and stick a white sugar pearl in each one.

Roll the remaining black fondant icing into a ball and shape into a rounded triangular nose shape. Position onto the cake above the cheeks.

Mould two ears out of the yellow fondant icing, pushing your thumb into the icing to create an ear cavity. Set aside.

Fill the pastry/piping bag with the chocolate and hazelnut spread. Pipe a 1-cm/³/₈-inch circle of hairs around the edge of the cake, then complete another two circles inside the one before it, creating a complete mane approximately 3 cm/1¹/₄ inches in width from the edge of the cake. Insert two wooden skewers into the base of each ear and use to secure them in place at the top of the lion's head, on the sides of the cake.

INDIAN ELEPHANT

Take a walk on the wide side of baking and create this big and beautifully decorated elephant cake. As with a lot of cakes in this book, you might wish to bake it before the day you plan to decorate it, as it requires cutting to an animal shape. Finally, get creative and decorate the serving plate with Indian-style sequins and jewels to complete the theme.

1 quantity Extra Large Basic
   Vanilla Cake mixture
   (see page 11)
1 quantity Vanilla Buttercream
   (see page 20)
black and red gel or paste food
   colouring
black, white, red and yellow
   writing icing
silver and coloured sugar pearls
coloured sweets/candies
33 x 23 x 6-cm/13 x 9 x 2½-inch
   cake pan, greased and lined
   with baking parchment
paper template of an elephant the
   same size as the cake pan (draw
   freehand and cut out with scissors
   or search online for 2D elephant
   pictures to print and cut out)
pastry/piping bag, fitted with a small
   star-shaped nozzle/tip, or make
   your own (see page 29)

Serves 12

Preheat the oven to 180°C (350°F) Gas 4.

Make the vanilla cake mixture and spoon into the prepared cake pan. Bake on the middle shelf of the preheated oven for 40 minutes until an inserted skewer comes out clean. Cool for 10 minutes in the pans, then remove to cool completely on a wire rack. If you have time, wrap the cold cake in clingfilm/plastic wrap and refrigerate overnight before continuing.

When you are ready to assemble the cake, take your elephant template, lay on top of the cake and, using a small, sharp knife, carefully cut around the paper template. Use the leftover bits of cake for a trifle, in lunchboxes or to snack on.

Reserve one-quarter of the buttercream and set aside. Tint the remaining buttercream grey using black food colouring. Coat the whole cake with the buttercream, spreading evenly with a palette knife/metal spatula.

Put 3–4 tablespoons of the reserved buttercream in a small bowl and tint it red. Fill the pastry/piping bag with the buttercream and use to pipe rosettes in the shape of a cap on the elephant's head. Use the remaining plain buttercream to make a leaf-shaped saddle on the elephant's back. Use the different writing icings to pipe decorative lines over the legs, trunk and neck, and as tassels below the saddle. Use the white writing icing to fill in the tusk. Decorate the elephant with silver and coloured sugar pearls, and use the sweets/candies to line the saddle.

TEDDY BEAR

Not the scary-looking grizzly bear you might think of in the wild, this cute teddy bear cake is perfect for a younger child. To make the ears and nose, you will need to make a batch of cupcakes, but since you only need a small number of them for the teddy bear cake, the remaining cupcakes can either be frozen for another time or coated with frosting as on page 66 and served alongside the teddy.

1 quantity Large Basic Vanilla or Chocolate Cake mixture (see page 11)
1 quantity Small Basic Vanilla or Chocolate Cake mixture (see page 11)
1 quantity Chocolate Fudge Frosting (see page 21)
assorted chocolate drops and buttons
ribbon
2 x 20-cm/8-inch cake pans, greased and lined with baking parchment
12-hole muffin pan, lined with 6 cupcake cases and 1 mini cupcake case

Serves 10

Preheat the oven to 180°C (350°F) Gas 4.

Make the vanilla cake mixtures in separate bowls and spoon the large quantity into the prepared cake pans and divide the small quantity between the cupcake cases. Bake on the middle shelf of the preheated oven until an inserted skewer comes out clean – 30 minutes for the cakes, 25 minutes for the cupcakes and 15 minutes for the mini cupcake. Cool for 10 minutes in the pans, then remove to cool completely on a wire rack.

If necessary, trim the tops of the cakes to make them level. Sandwich together using 3–4 tablespoons of chocolate fudge frosting – the bottom side of the top cake should be facing up. Use three-quarters of the remaining frosting to coat the top and sides of the whole cake, spreading evenly with a palette knife/metal spatula.

Peel the cupcake case off one cupcake and cut the cupcake in half horizontally. Position one half on each side of the head to make the ears. Coat the tops of two other cupcakes with frosting and place on top of the halved cupcakes so that they are roughly level with the top of the teddy's face.

Peel the cupcake case off the mini cupcake and completely coat the cupcake with frosting. Position upside-down in the middle of the cake to make the teddy's nose. Arrange the chocolate drops on the face for the eyes, mouth and ear cavities. Make a bow out of the ribbon and place at the teddy's neck.

On the rare chance you'd see a sloth awake from its slumber, it would surely look as cute and wide-eyed as this smiling character here!

SMILING SLOTH

1 quantity Extra Large Basic Vanilla
   Cake mixture plus 1 quantity
   of Small Vanilla Cake mixture
   (see page 11 and make up the
   two mixtures together)
1¹/₂ quantities Vanilla Buttercream
   (see page 20)

TO DECORATE
25 g/1 oz. white flower
   modelling paste
black and pink gel or paste food
   colouring
icing/confectioners' sugar,
   for dusting
120 g/4 oz. grey fondant icing
190 g/6³/₄ oz. white fondant icing
35 g/1¹/₄ oz. brown fondant icing
25 g/1 oz. black fondant icing
6 white sugar pearls
14 cocktail sticks/toothpicks
2-litre/2-quart/8-cup round Pyrex
   bowl, greased with sunflower
   oil and base-lined with a
   10-cm/4-inch disc of baking
   parchment
3 x 18-cm/7-inch cake pans,
   greased and lined with
   baking parchment
14-cm/5¹/₂-inch round
   pastry/cookie cutter
2.5-cm/1-inch round
   pastry/cookie cutter
thin paintbrush
2-cm/³/₄-inch round
   pastry/cookie cutter

Serves 28–30

Start with the claws. Divide the white modelling paste into 12 pieces. Roll out each into a pointed sausage shape of 3 cm/1¹/₄ inches long. Cut six cocktail sticks/toothpicks in half, brush the pointed ends with water and push into the flat side of the claws. Leave to set for at least 2 hours.

Pour 450 g/1 lb of the cake mixture into the Pyrex bowl and cook in a microwave on high at 800W for 5–6 minutes until an inserted skewer comes out clean. Carefully remove from the microwave and turn out onto a wire rack to cool. If necessary, trim the base of the dome to make it level.

Preheat the oven to 180°C (350°F) Gas 4. Divide the remaining mixture between the prepared cake pans. Bake in the oven for 35–40 minutes or until an inserted skewer comes out clean. Leave the cakes to cool in their pans for 10 minutes, then turn out onto a wire rack to cool completely.

Sandwich together the cakes – domed cake on top – using 450 g/1 lb of the buttercream. Place on a serving plate and crumb-coat (see page 27) using 450 g/1 lb buttercream. Chill for 15 minutes. Place the remaining buttercream in a bowl and tint it grey using the black colouring. Coat the cake in a second layer, applying loosely with a small palette knife/metal spatula to create fur. Take a few pinches of the grey fondant icing and place on top of the head.

For the face, dust a surface with icing/confectioners' sugar and roll out 150 g/5¹/₂ oz. white icing to 3 mm/¹/₈ inch thick. Use the largest cutter to cut a circle (reserve trimmings). Gently press onto the buttercream. Divide the brown icing in two and roll out to 2 mm/¹/₁₆ inch thick rectangles. Use a knife to round off a short side of each rectangle. Brush one side of each with water and stick to the white fondant so the rounded sides face in, then trim the outer edges, flush with the circle. Roll out the remaining white icing to 2 mm/¹/₁₆ inch thick. Cut out two circles using the medium-sized cutter (reserve trimmings). Brush one side of each with water and stick to the tops of the rectangles. Repeat with the black icing, trimming slightly, and stick to the white circles. Cut out a circle using the same cutter, and cut into it to create a crescent-shaped mouth. Use the trimmings to mould a small nose. Stick both in position using a little water. Make three divots in each eye with a paintbrush end, brush with a little water and place in white sugar pearls. For the cheeks, tint the remaining white icing pink and roll out and cut to the same size as the whites of the eyes. Brush one side of each with water and stick in position.

Divide the remaining grey fondant into four and shape into blocks. Insert two cocktail sticks/toothpicks into one of the widest sides of each of the blocks. Push the claws into place at the front of each, then insert two blocks in each side of the cake to create arms and legs.

SNAKE IN THE GRASS

1 quantity Large Basic Vanilla
   or Chocolate Cake mixture
   (see page 11)
1 quantity Vanilla Buttercream
   (see page 20)

TO DECORATE
green, red, yellow gel or paste
   food colouring
300 g/10½ oz. black fondant icing
175 g/6 oz. red Smarties/
   candy-coated chocolates
2 white chocolate drops
1 black writing icing pen
1 red liquorice belt, with a triangle
   shape snipped out of one end
24-cm/9½-inch bundt pan
muffin pan, lined with
   2 cupcake cases
pastry/piping bag, fitted with
   a 1-cm/⅜-inch round piping
   nozzle/tip, or make your own
   (see page 29)
thin paintbrush

FOR THE GRASSY BOARD
50 g/1¾ oz. green flower
   modelling paste
green cake board (approximately
   35 x 45 cm/14 x 18 inches)
pastry/piping bag, fitted with
   a grass-shaped nozzle/tip
30 g/1½ packed cups fresh
   mint leaves
2 Oreo cookies, whizzed in
   a food processor

Serves 16

First, make the grass. Roll out the green modelling paste to 2 mm/¹⁄₁₆ inch thick on baking parchment. Cut out six 6-cm/2½-inch squares, then thin grass shapes from one side of each square. Loosely wrap around wooden spoon handles. Slightly bend the blades as liked. Leave to set for 1–2 hours.

Preheat the oven to 180°C (350°F) Gas 4. Divide 100 g/3½ oz. of the cake mixture between the cupcake cases and place the remaining mixture in the bundt pan. Bake until an inserted skewer comes out clean – 20 minutes for the cupcakes and 35 minutes for the bundt. Cool for 10 minutes in the pans, then remove to cool completely on a wire rack. Cut the bundt in half crossways and turn to make an 'S' shape. Place the cupcakes at either end and trim the sides of one cupcake to make a tail. Sit the trimmings either side of the second cake to make the head. Secure together with a little buttercream, then coat in a thin layer, just past the joins, using 75 g/2⅔ oz. buttercream.

In a bowl, tint 100 g/3½ oz. of the buttercream green, cover and set aside. Put 125 g/4½ oz. of the buttercream in another bowl and tint bright red. Put the remaining buttercream in a third bowl and tint bright yellow. Using all the red buttercream and 125 g/4½ oz. of the yellow, coat the body in a thin layer of buttercream. Starting with red next to the head, alternate the colours every 6 cm/2½ inches, finishing with yellow next to the cupcake tail.

Dust a surface with icing/confectioners' sugar and roll out the black icing to 3 mm/⅛ inch thick. Cut a 15 x 17-cm/6 x 6¾-inch rectangle. Use a rolling pin to drape over the head; smooth down to cover. Trim the excess icing from the base. Re-roll the trimmings and cut a 13 x 15-cm/5¼ x 6-inch rectangle and repeat as above to cover the tip of the tail. Re-roll the trimmings to 2 mm/¹⁄₁₆ inch thick, cut seven 1.5 x 16-cm/⅝ x 6¼-inch strips and set aside.

To cover the yellow undercoat, start from the tail end. Put the remaining yellow buttercream in the pastry/piping bag with the round nozzle/tip. Pipe on blobs of buttercream in rows and once you get to the red undercoat, lay over a strip of black fondant icing to create a seam, then cover the red buttercream with the red Smarties/candy-coated chocolates. Lay them side-by-side, as close as you can. Repeat until the snake's body is covered.

For eyes, make indentations on the head with a paintbrush end. Brush with a little water and stick in white chocolate drops. Use the black icing pen to draw pupils. Mark a mouth-shape with a knife and insert the straight liquorice end to create a tongue. Fill the pastry/piping bag with the grass nozzle/tip with the green buttercream. Pipe little tufts of grass around the snake and insert grass from step one and the mint. Scatter the Oreo crumbs for earth.

ZANY ZEBRA

1 quantity medium Basic Vanilla
  Cake mixture (see page 11,
  but made with 250 ml/1 cup
  vegetable oil instead of butter)
1 quantity medium Basic Chocolate
  Cake mixture (see page 11,
  but made with 250 ml/1 cup
  vegetable oil instead of butter)
1 quantity Vanilla Buttercream
  (see page 20, but made with
  white vegetable fat, such as Trex
  or Cookeen, instead of butter)

TO DECORATE
70 g/2½ oz. white flower
  modelling paste
icing/confectioners' sugar,
  plus extra for dusting
25 g/1 oz. pink fondant icing
black gel or paste food colouring
200g/7 oz. black fondant icing
2 Minstrels or brown M&M's
*2 x 23-cm/9-inch round cake pans,
  greased and lined with
  baking parchment*
*3-cm/1¼-inch round
  pastry/cookie cutter*
4 small wooden skewers
*7-cm/2¾-inch round
  pastry/cookie cutter*
*2.5-cm/1-inch round
  pastry/cookie cutter*
*2-cm/¾-inch round
  pastry/cookie cutter*

Serves 28–30

Start with the ears. Divide the white modelling paste into two pieces; roll each into a short cone. Dust a surface with icing/confectioners' sugar and gently using a rolling pin, slightly flatten. Roll out the pink fondant to 2 mm/¹/₁₆ inch thick and use the 3-cm/1¼-inch cutter to stamp out two circles for the inner ear (reserve the trimmings). Brush one side with a little water and stick to the white outer ear. Push your thumb into the icing to create an ear cavity. Dip one end of the small skewers in water and insert two in the base of each ear. Leave to set for at least 2 hours.

Preheat the oven to 180°C (350°F) Gas 4.

Stir the black food colouring through the chocolate mix to get a dark brown–black colour. Using a small ladle, drop alternate equal ladlefuls of the two cake mixtures into the prepared cake pans. Then, for each, put a skewer in the middle of the cake pan and drag it from the middle outwards, along the edge and then back into the middle. Repeat to create a flower-pattern in the mixture. Bake for 35–40 minutes until an inserted skewer comes out clean. Cool for 10 minutes in the pans, then turn out onto a wire rack to completely.

If necessary, trim the tops of the cakes to make them level. Sandwich together using 200 g/7 oz. of the buttercream – the bottom side of the top cake should be facing up. Place on a cake plate and crumb-coat (see page 27) the cake using 350 g/12 oz. of the buttercream. Chill for 15 minutes. Use the remaining buttercream to coat the cake in a second layer. Smooth and remove the excess buttercream with a palette knife/metal spatula.

Dust a surface with icing/confectioners' sugar and roll out the black fondant icing to 3 mm/⅛ inch thick. For the snout, cut a 16 x 6.5-cm/6¼ x 2½-inch rectangle, then 'round-off' the edges using a knife. Place on top of the cake. Cut out a large circle using the largest cutter. Using a knife, cut wiggly-pointy strips into one side to create a fringe/bangs, then stick to the buttercream in the middle of the top edge of the cake. Use the 2.5-cm/1-inch cutter to cut two circles for the eyes and stick into position. Brush with a little water and gently press the Minstrels or brown M&M's on top, for pupils.

Using a knife, cut wiggly-pointy strips – between 5 cm/2 inches and 10 cm/4 inches long – from the remaining black fondant, and arrange around the edge of the zebra face and sides of the cake. Roll out the pink trimmings. Use the 2-cm/¾-inch cutter to cut out two circles for the nostrils. Use the 2.5-cm/1-inch cutter to cut out a circle for the mouth, and cut into it to create a crescent-shaped mouth. Brush one side of each shape with water and position on the cake. Just before serving, push the ears into position.

2 quantities Large Basic Vanilla mixture (see page 11) baked in two 23-cm/9-inch greased and lined deep cake pans for 45 minutes, until an inserted skewer comes out clean, then cooled

1 quantity Extra Large Basic Vanilla mixture (see page 11) baked in three 18-cm/7-inch cake pans for 35–40 minutes, until an inserted skewer comes out clean, then cooled

2 quantities Vanilla Buttercream (see page 20)

TO DECORATE
icing/confectioners' sugar, for dusting
50 g/1¾ oz. green flower modelling paste
edible silver lustre
160 g/5⅔ oz. medium pink flower modelling paste
15 g/½ oz. pastel pink flower modelling paste
10 g/⅓ oz. lemon yellow flower modelling paste
black food colouring pen
blue gel or paste food colouring
300 g/10½ oz. very pale pink fondant icing
160 g/5⅔ oz. very pale pink flower modelling paste
150 g/5½ oz. dark pink flower modelling paste
edible glue
2 chocolate wafer rolls
fake lily-style bright flowers
2 tropical leaf pastry/cookie cutters
3 short, thin wooden skewers
cocktail stick/toothpick
4 cake dowels
small flower pastry/cookie cutter
18-cm/7-inch cake board
pink ribbon
2 'firework' cocktail sticks/toothpicks

Serves 50

TROPICAL FLAMINGO

Start with the decoration. Dust a surface and roll the green modelling paste thinly. Stamp out four leaves using the leaf cutters. Drape over a small rolling pin to create wavy shapes. Brush with edible silver lustre. For the flamingo, roll the medium pink modelling paste into an elongated cone shape, one end slightly bigger for the head. Gently roll a rolling pin over it to flatten slightly, pinching the end of the body to create a 'tail feather'. Bend into a number '2' shape. Lay on baking parchment. For the wing, roll the pastel pink modelling paste to 2 mm/1/16 inch thick. Stamp out a half-flower using the flower cutter. Brush one side with a little water and drape over the flamingo's body. For the beak, take the yellow modelling paste and roll into a cone-shape. Leave each piece to set overnight. Colour the beak tip black with the food colouring pen.

If necessary, trim the tops of the cakes to make them level. Sandwich together the smaller cakes using 300 g/10½ oz. buttercream – the bottom side of the top cake should be facing up. Secure on the cake board with a little buttercream and crumb-coat (see page 27) using 400 g/14 oz. buttercream. Chill for 15 minutes. Place 600 g/21½ oz. buttercream in a bowl and tint it turquoise blue. Use to coat the cake in a second layer of buttercream. Smooth and remove the excess with a palette knife/metal spatula. Sandwich together the larger cakes using 200 g/7 oz. plain buttercream. Place on a cake plate and use the remaining buttercream to crumb-coat. Dust a surface and roll out the very pale pink fondant icing to a 30-cm/12-inch circle, 3 mm/1/8 inch thick. Use a rolling pin to drape it over the top and a small way down the large cake. Smooth down.

For the ruffles, dust a work surface and roll the very pale pink modelling paste into 15 g/1/2 oz. sausage shapes. Roll thinly with a rolling pin. Stick where the buttercream meets the fondant icing. Repeat with another row of very pale pink beneath it, then medium pink, then two final rows of dark pink.

Construct the cake. Cut the dowels to the height of the large cake. Push them into the cake to form a square and sit the smaller cake on top. Position the ribbon; secure in place by inserting a cocktail stick/toothpick in the back seam. Very gently flip over the flamingo, brush the skewers with edible glue and insert into the body. Repeat with the cocktail stick/toothpick for the head. Brush the back of the flamingo with edible glue and stick to the front of the cake. Brush the beak with edible glue and position. Roll a small piece of dark pink modelling paste to fill between the beak and head. Brush with edible glue. Use the food colouring pen to draw an eye. For the legs, roll the dark pink modelling paste into two thin pieces and position. Place the firework cocktail sticks/toothpicks in the chocolate wafer rolls for 'palm trees' and add to the cake with the lily-style flowers and prepared green leaves.

CUDDLY PENGUINS

Whoever would have thought that lurking under these bobble hats are cupcakes?
Usually found waddling towards feeding time at the zoo, here they're shuffling
through crushed-up meringues – perfect for creating a snowy, polar theme.

1 quantity Buttermilk Cake
(see page 12)
1 quantity Vanilla Buttercream
(see page 20)

TO DECORATE
black, yellow and red gel or paste
food colouring
tiny white chocolate drops
125 g/4 oz. white fondant icing
ready-made meringues (optional),
to decorate a serving dish
icing/confectioners' sugar,
for dusting

muffin pan, lined with
8–10 cupcake cases
mini-muffin pan, lined with
8–10 small cupcake cases
in the coordinating sizes
2 cocktail sticks/toothpicks

Makes 8–10

Preheat the oven to 180°C (350°F) Gas 4.

Divide the cake mixture between the cupcake cases, filling them two-thirds full, and bake on the middle shelf of the preheated oven for 12–25 minutes. The time will vary according to the size of the cakes – keep an eye on them and take them out when they are well risen and a skewer inserted into the middle of the cakes comes out clean. Cool for 5 minutes in the pans, then remove to cool completely on a wire rack.

Put two-thirds of the buttercream in a bowl and tint it black using the food colouring. Leave the rest of the buttercream plain.

Next, make the penguins. Remove the cupcake cases from all the cold cupcakes and trim the top off each to make level. Lay the larger cupcakes upside down on a clean work surface and dab a little of the buttercream on the top. Lay a mini cupcake upside down on top of each larger cupcake. Using a palette knife/metal spatula, spread the black buttercream smoothly all over the penguins, leaving an area for the tummy. Spread the plain buttercream into the tummy area. Press two tiny white chocolate drops onto each penguin's face for the eyes. Using a cocktail stick/toothpick, dab a little black food colouring onto the middle of each eye.

To make the beaks, take 25 g/1 oz. of the fondant icing and tint it yellow using the food colouring. Break off small nuggets of the icing and shape into triangles for the beaks. Stick one onto the front of each penguin.

To make the wings, tint half of the remaining icing black using the food colouring. Pinch off hazelnut-sized pieces and shape and flatten into wings. Press one wing onto each side of each penguin. Use the remaining icing to make the bobble hats. Tint three-quarters of it red and leave the remainder white. Roll and pinch the red icing into cone shapes and push the ends so that they droop. Roll the white icing into small balls and prick each one all over with a cocktail stick/toothpick to make it look like a pompom. Stick one to the end of each hat. Carefully place a hat on top of each penguin.

Crush the meringues and scatter over a serving dish, if you like. Dust with icing/confectioners' sugar and add the penguins to the snow scene.

TEDDY BEAR CUPCAKES

Perfect for serving alongside the Teddy Bear Cake on page 54, everything you need to make these cute teddy bears can be found in the baking or confectionery aisle of the supermarket. Kids love them and they'll get particularly excited if you let them stick the decorations on!

1 quantity Chocolate Cupcakes (see page 15)
1 quantity Chocolate Meringue Buttercream (see page 21)
chocolate sprinkles or finely grated/shredded chocolate
24 giant milk chocolate buttons
24 white chocolate buttons
12 regular milk chocolate buttons
36 brown candy-coated chocolate drops
chocolate writing icing or 50 g/1¾ oz. dark/bittersweet chocolate, melted
muffin pan, lined with brown cupcake cases

Makes 12

Preheat the oven to 180°C (350°F) Gas 4.

Prepare and bake the chocolate cupcakes. Allow them to rest in the pan for 3–4 minutes, then transfer to a wire rack and allow to cool completely.

Prepare the chocolate meringue buttercream. Using a small palette knife/metal spatula, coat the top of each cooled cupcake with chocolate meringue buttercream and scatter an even layer of chocolate sprinkles or grated chocolate over the top to create fur.

Lay the giant chocolate buttons on the work surface and dab the top of each with a dot of buttercream. Lay the white buttons on top and press together. Position 2 pairs of buttons at the top of each cupcake for ears. Lay the regular milk chocolate buttons on the work surface, dab the underside of 12 of the chocolate drops with buttercream and press one onto each of the chocolate buttons. Dab a little more buttercream on the underside of each button and position as a nose on the cupcakes. Position the remaining chocolate drops as eyes and use the writing icing (or melted chocolate) to draw a mouth. Your teddies are now ready to serve.

ANIMAL-FACE CUPCAKES

Here's an idea for the child in all of us! You can really go to town with the decorating and pick any animal that has distinctive enough features to represent in sprinkles, candies and frosting. Here is a monkey, bear, rabbit and pig, but the choice is yours.

1 quantity Buttermilk Cake
　　mixture (see page 12)
1 quantity Meringue Buttercream
　　(see page 21)

TO DECORATE
assorted gel or paste food
　　colouring
75 g/2¹/₂ oz. dark/bittersweet
　　chocolate, chopped
marshmallows in assorted
　　sizes and colours
jelly beans in assorted colours
liquorice shoelaces
white, milk and dark/bittersweet
　　chocolate buttons in assorted
　　sizes
chocolate sprinkles and
　　other-coloured sprinkles
white sugar strands or nonpareils
¹/₂ quantity Royal Icing
　　(see page 22)
1–2 muffin pans, lined with
　　cupcake cases
small pastry/piping bag, fitted with
　　a fine writing nozzle/tip, or make
　　your own (see page 29)

Makes 12–16

Preheat the oven to 180°C (350°F) Gas 4.

Divide the buttermilk cake mixture between the cupcake cases, filling them two-thirds full, and bake on the middle shelf of the preheated oven for 20 minutes or until well risen and an inserted skewer comes out clean. Cool for 5 minutes in the pans, then remove to cool completely on a wire rack.

How you decorate these cupcakes depends on the animals you have chosen. These are just tips for making facial features.

Tint the meringue buttercream into as many different colours as you need by dividing it between separate bowls and tinting each one using food colouring.

To make a bear, monkey or any other brown animal face, put the chocolate in a heatproof bowl set over a pan of barely simmering water. Stir until smooth and melted. Add to one bowl of meringue buttercream and stir until well mixed. Coat the tops of the cold cupcakes in your tinted buttercream, spreading smoothly with a palette knife/metal spatula.

Use marshmallows in assorted sizes to make noses and snouts. Coat with tinted buttercream to match the rest of the face and push into the face to attach. You can also cut a large marshmallow in half and pinch or squash with your fingers to shape into ears. Stick at the top of the cupcake.

Use halved jelly beans for nostrils or large eyes. Strips of liquorice positioned under the nose make good mouths or whiskers.

Use white, milk and dark/bittersweet chocolate buttons, individually or stacked, for ears. Stick in place with a dab of buttercream.

Chocolate sprinkles and other-coloured sprinkles and nonpareils make ideal fur. While sugar strands can be used for buck teeth.

Complete the features with thinly piped black royal icing to make little eyes and dainty smiles or just to glue features in place.

TEDDY BEAR GINGERBREAD

Look for sets of teddy-bear cutters in assorted sizes so that you can make a whole family of teddy bears. These teddy bears are brown, but you could turn them into snowy polar bears, if you prefer.

**Basic Spiced Gingerbread
(see page 18)**
**plain/all-purpose flour,
for dusting**
Royal Icing (see page 22)
**brown, black and pink gel
or paste food colouring**
*teddy-bear cutters in three
different sizes*
*baking sheets, lined with
baking parchment*
*pastry/piping bag or make
your own (see page 29)*

Makes 10–12

Prepare the basic spiced gingerbread, stopping at the end of Step 3. Preheat the oven to 160°C (325°F) Gas 3.

Lightly dust a clean surface with flour and roll the dough evenly to a thickness of 3 mm/¹/₈ inch. Use the cutters to stamp out as many cookies as possible from the dough, cutting each one as close as possible to the next one. Arrange the cookies on the prepared baking sheets. Gather the dough scraps together, knead lightly, re-roll and stamp out more cookies until all the dough has been used up. Bake the gingerbread in batches on the middle shelf of the preheated oven for 10–12 minutes or until firm and lightly browned at the edges. Allow the cookies to cool completely on the baking sheets before icing.

Prepare the royal icing. Put half the icing in one bowl, one quarter in a second bowl and the last quarter in a third bowl. Tint the largest bowl of icing light brown using the food colouring. Tint the second bowl black and the remaining bowl pink. Cover and set aside.

Take 3 tablespoons of brown icing and add a little more colour to make it a deeper brown. Fill a pastry/piping bag with this darker colour and pipe outlines around the edge of each bear. (See page 22 for instructions on flooding.) Allow to dry for at least 10 minutes. Flood the insides of the outlines with paler brown icing. Allow to dry for 20 minutes. Pipe paws and ears onto each bear with the darker brown icing. Pipe the eyes, nose and mouth onto each bear using the black icing in another pastry/piping bag. Finish by putting the pink icing in another pastry/piping bag and piping a bow tie on each bear. Allow to dry completely before serving.

ON THE *Farm*

FLUFFY SHEEP

This cake is so simple to make it's BAA-rmy, and can be easily baked on the day of the party. You need only one cupcake, so freeze the rest for another time.

1 quantity Large Basic Vanilla Cake mixture (see page 11)

1 quantity Small Basic Vanilla Cake mixture (see page 11)

1 quantity Vanilla Buttercream (see page 20)

600 g/1 lb. 5 oz. white mini marshmallows

2 pink regular marshmallows

chocolate sprinkles

2 chocolate drops

black writing icing

2-litre/2-quart/8-cup round Pyrex bowl, greased with sunflower woil and dusted with flour

6-hole muffin pan, lined with cupcake cases

4 cocktail sticks/toothpicks

Serves 10–12

Preheat the oven to 180°C (350°F) Gas 4.

Make the vanilla cake mixtures separately and spoon the large quantity into the prepared bowl and divide the small quantity between the cupcake cases. Bake on the middle shelf of the preheated oven until an inserted skewer comes out clean – 1 hour for the cake and 20–25 minutes for the cupcakes. Cool for 10 minutes in the bowl and pans, then remove to cool completely on a wire rack. If necessary, trim the tops of the cakes to make them level. Put the cake, flat-side down, on a serving plate and coat it with the buttercream, spreading evenly with a palette knife/metal spatula.

Peel the cupcake case off one cupcake (and freeze the rest of the cupcakes to use another time). Coat the cupcake with buttercream, position on top of the sheep for the head and secure in place with a cocktail stick/toothpick.

Cover the body and the head of the sheep with the mini marshmallows, leaving a space for the sheep's face. Carefully coat a regular marshmallow with buttercream and stick to the face. Secure in place with a cocktail stick/toothpick.

Cover the face and nose with chocolate sprinkles and press to stick.

Cut the remaining regular marshmallow in half, pinch the ends together to make ear shapes and attach to the sides of the head with cocktail sticks/toothpicks.

Using the black writing icing, pipe a nose and mouth on the face and use to attach chocolate drop eyes.

DELILAH THE COW

Pull the udder one! This cake makes the
most of some candy favourites.

1 quantity Extra Large Basic
Chocolate Cake mixture
(see page 11) ½ of the mixture
baked in a 23-cm/9-inch greased
and lined cake pan, the other
½ of the mixture baked in a
20 cm/8-inch greased and lined
cake pan, for 35–40 minutes,
until an inserted skewer comes
out clean, then cooled
1 quantity Vanilla Buttercream
(see page 20)

TO DECORATE
7 Oreo cookies
2 almond cantucci cookies
4 tablespoons icing/confectioners'
sugar, plus extra for dusting
60 g/2 oz. light pink fondant icing
4 light pink jelly beans
2 dark pink jelly beans
2 brown Smarties/candy-coated
chocolates
cake board, at least
36 cm/14 inches long
paper or thin card

Serves 20

Start with the cake. If necessary, trim the tops of the cakes to make them level. Place the larger cake flat-side up on the cake board. Secure in place with a little buttercream. For the cow's head, take the smaller cake and cut a strip from the middle, about 12 cm/4³/₄ inches wide at the top, tapering to about 4 cm/1½ inches at the base. Trim to make the shape of the cow's head. Cut across the remaining two side panels, slightly on the diagonal, to make two ears and two 10 cm/4 inch legs. Set aside.

Place 400 g/14 oz. of the buttercream in a bowl to use for sandwiching the cakes together and then crumb-coat (see page 27). Spread buttercream on the base of the head and ears and stick to the top edge of the larger cake, following the curve, then crumb-coat the whole cake.

Place the cut-out leg cake pieces into position and trim the tops, flush to the cake. Secure in place and crumb-coat with buttercream. Chill for 20 minutes.

Use a dinner knife or small palette knife/metal spatula to apply a second coat all over the cake, using the remaining buttercream. Smooth over.

Attach two of the Oreo cookies to the cake for hooves. Whizz the remainder in a food processor until you have fine crumbs. Sprinkle over the cake in spots, avoiding the base of snout. Press the cantucci cookies into the top of the head for horns.

For the snout and udder, cut two oval shapes out of paper or thin card to use as templates, one approximately 9 x 5 cm/3½ x 2 inches and the other 8 x 3 cm/3¼ x 1¼ inches. Dust a surface with icing/confectioners' sugar and roll out the pink icing to 3 mm/¹/₈ inch thick. Use the templates to cut out two oval shapes. Brush one side of the larger piece with a little water and stick to the cake for the snout. Repeat for the smaller piece and stick to the edge of the cake for the udder.

In a small bowl, mix together the icing/confectioners' sugar with about ½–1 teaspoon water until you have a smooth glacé icing.

Make four little divots in the udder using one of the jelly beans, dot the divots with a little glacé icing, and then secure the light pink jelly beans in place. For the nostrils, press the dark pink jelly beans in place. Finally, for the eyes, stick the Smarties/candy-coated chocolates in place, onto the buttercream.

PRIZE-WINNING HORSE

1 quantity Extra Large Basic Vanilla
   Cake mixture (see page 11) baked
   in three 18-cm/7-inch greased
   and lined round cake pans for
   35–40 minutes, until an inserted
   skewer comes out clean, then
   cooled
1½ quantities Vanilla Buttercream
   (see page 20)

TO DECORATE
175 g/6 oz. white flower
   modelling paste
icing/confectioners' sugar,
   for dusting
25 g/1 oz. grey flower
   modelling paste
2 black sugar pearls
turquoise-blue gel or paste
   food colouring
150 g/5 oz. white fondant icing
16 ready-made sugar-paste
   flowers in various sizes
   (optional)
35 g/1¼ oz. green flower
   modelling paste
40 g/1½ oz. pink flower
   modelling paste
thin paintbrush
thin sharp knife or fondant knife
4.5-cm/1¾-inch round
   pastry/cookie cutter
5-cm/2-inch fluted
   pastry/cookie cutter
cocktail stick/toothpick
number badge – pin sterilized
   in hot water (approximately
   4 cm/1½ inches in diameter)

Serves 20

Start with the white modelling paste for the horse. For the body, roll 65 g/2 oz. into a flat-based rounded cone. For back legs, roll 10 g/⅓ oz. pieces into small cones. Slightly flatten the large end. For front legs, roll 8 g/¼ oz. pieces into sausage shapes to the size of the body. Brush one side of each leg with a little water and attach to the body. Use a knife to mark the end of each leg for hooves. For the head, roll 40 g/1½ oz. into a small cone. Dust a surface and roll the grey modelling paste to 2 mm/1/16 inch thick. Use the round cutter to stamp out a circle (reserve the trimmings). Brush one side with a little water and press to the larger cone end. Using the paintbrush end, make two divots for the nostrils. Repeat for eyes, brush with a little water and add black sugar pearls. Add lashes and a smile with a knife. Insert a cocktail stick/toothpick into the top of the body. Brush with a little water and push on the head. For ears, roll two small balls from the white modelling paste, mould to triangles, brush with a little water and stick to the head. For the mane and tail, take pea-sized pieces of the grey modelling paste, roll into thin strips and twist, brush with water and stick in place. Leave to dry.

If necessary, trim the tops of the cakes to make level. Sandwich together using 300 g/10½ oz. buttercream – the bottom side of the top cake should be facing up. Place on a cake plate and crumb-coat (see page 27) using 400 g/14 oz. buttercream. Chill for 15 minutes. Tint 250 g/9 oz. buttercream turquoise, the remaining a lighter shade. Use a dinner knife to coat the bottom half of the cake in the darker shade; top half in the lighter shade, blending in the middle. Smooth and remove the excess buttercream with a palette knife/metal spatula.

For the fence, dust a surface and roll out the white fondant icing to 2 mm/1/16 inch thick. Cut out seven 8 cm/3¼ inch long 'posts' and fourteen 10-cm/4-inch 'horizontal slats' (reserve the trimmings). Press onto the cake, brushing with a little water to help stick. Place the horse on the top of the cake. For grass tufts, roll the green modelling paste as above. Cut out 12 small rectangles. Slice into the tops and pinch together at the bottom (reserve the trimmings). Press around the base and top of the cake.

For the rosette, roll 25 g/1 oz. pink modelling paste into a long sausage, then to 2 mm/1/16-inch thick. Bend it round into a 7-cm/2¾-inch circle, pleating as you go. Join the seam, trim and set aside. For a ribbon, cut two strips from the pink and green trimmings. Press the green strips onto the buttercream near the base of the cake – the rosette just above – then stick the pink strips on top using a little water. Roll the remaining white icing to 3 mm/1/8 inch thick. Stamp a circle using the fluted cutter, brush one side with a little water and stick to the rosette. Push the badge into the icing and remove before slicing.

This delightful horse is star
of the country fair. Be extra creative
and use a little water to stick
on ready-made sugar-paste
flowers, or add rustic
details to the fence
with a paintbrush end.

Cool inside and out, this surprise-inside blue cake is a must for any chilled llama fan!

1 quantity Extra Large Basic Vanilla
   Cake mixture plus 1 quantity
   of Small Vanilla Cake mixture
   (see page 11 and make up the
   two mixtures together, and
   tint with blue gel or paste food
   colouring)
2 quantities Vanilla Buttercream
   (see page 20)

TO DECORATE
icing/confectioners' sugar,
   for dusting
60 g/2 oz. white flower
   modelling paste
35 g/1¹⁄₄ oz. pink flower
   modelling paste
100 g/3¹⁄₂ oz. white fondant icing
30 g/1 oz. light blue flower
   modelling paste
30 g/1 oz. dark blue flower
   modelling paste
black writing icing pen
8 x 5-cm/3¹⁄₄ x 2-inch leaf
   pastry/cookie cutter
6 x 3.5-cm/2¹⁄₂ x 1¹⁄₂-inch leaf
   pastry/cookie cutter
2-litre/2-quart/8-cup round Pyrex
   bowl, greased with sunflower
   oil and base-lined with
   a 10-cm/4-inch disc of
   baking parchment
3 x 18-cm/7-inch cake pans,
   greased and lined with
   baking parchment
14-cm/5¹⁄₂-inch round
   pastry/cookie cutter
6-cm/2¹⁄₂-inch star
   pastry/cookie cutter
4.5-cm/1³⁄₄-inch star
   pastry/cookie cutter
large pastry/piping bag, fitted with
   a large star nozzle/tip, or make
   your own (see page 29)

Serves 28–30

NO DRAMA LLAMA

First, make the ears. Dust a surface and roll out the white and the pink modelling paste to 2 mm/¹⁄₁₆ inch thick. Use the larger leaf cutter to cut out two pieces of white. Use the smaller leaf cutter to cut out two pieces of pink (reserve the white and pink trimmings). Brush one side of each pink leaf-shape with water and stick one to each of the white leaf-shapes. Pinch at the base of each to create the ear shape. Leave to set for at least 2 hours.

Preheat the oven to 180°C (350°F) Gas 4. Pour 450 g/1 lb of the cake mixture into the Pyrex bowl and cook in a microwave on high at 800W for 5–6 minutes until an inserted skewer comes out clean. Carefully remove from the microwave and turn out onto a wire rack to cool. If necessary, trim the base of the dome to make it level. Divide the remaining mix between the prepared cake pans. Bake for 35–40 minutes or until a skewer comes out clean. Cool for 10 minutes in the pans, then remove to cool completely on a wire rack.

If necessary, trim the tops of the cakes to make them level. Sandwich together the cakes – domed cake on top – using 450 g/1 lb of the buttercream. Place on a cake plate and crumb-coat (see page 27) using 450 g/1 lb of the buttercream. Chill for 15 minutes.

For the face, dust a surface and roll out the white fondant icing to 3 mm/¹⁄₈ inch thick. Use the round cutter to make a circle, then use the cutter to eclipse the circle to make a more oval shape. Brush one side with a little water and stick horizontally to the cake just below the dome shape. Use the reserved pink flower modelling paste to mould a small nose. Brush one side with a little water and stick into position.

For the sunglasses, dust a surface and roll out the light blue modelling paste to 2 mm/¹⁄₁₆ inch thick. Cut out two star shapes using the larger star cutter (reserve the trimmings). Repeat with the dark blue modelling paste using the smaller star cutter. Brush one side of the smaller stars with water and stick to the larger stars. Brush the backs with water and stick to the white icing face. Roll a pea-sized piece of the light blue modelling paste into a sausage shape. Brush one side with a little water and position as the glasses' bridge. Roll out the reserved white modelling paste to 2 mm/¹⁄₁₆ inch thick. Cut out two small triangles, brush one side of each with a little water and stick to sunglasses to create a 'shiny highlight'.

Fill the pastry/piping bag with the remaining buttercream and pipe stars around the white face, covering up the seam. Continue to coat the whole head, draw the buttercream slightly outwards and upwards to create a floppy fringe just above the face. Finally, put the ears into position and use the black writing icing pen to draw on the mouth.

RUBBER DUCKY CUPCAKES

These cute cupcakes will bring a smile to your face, just as little ducklings do when you see them at a farm. Each adorable 'rubber duck' has its own slightly quizzical expression as it bobs along on a sea of buttercream and bubbles. Make the ducks at least 24 hours in advance; you could also try making them from marzipan.

1 quantity **Vanilla Cupcakes**
   (see page 14)
1 quantity **Meringue Buttercream**
   (see page 21)

TO DECORATE
200 g/7 oz. ready-to-roll
   fondant icing
orange, yellow, black and blue gel
   or paste food colouring
blue and white sugar pearls
baking sheet, lined with
   baking parchment
wooden skewer
12-hole muffin pan, lined with
   cupcake cases
large pastry/piping bag, fitted with
   a large star-shaped nozzle/tip,
   or make your own (see page 29)

Makes 12

The day before you want to bake the cake, make the rubber duckies.

Knead a drop of the orange colouring into about 25 g/³/₄ oz. of the ready-to-roll icing. Repeat with the remaining icing using the yellow food colouring. Cover the orange icing in clingfilm/plastic wrap until ready to use.

Start by making the ducks' bodies. Divide the yellow icing in half and wrap one half in clingfilm/plastic wrap. Divide the other half into 12 pieces and roll into balls in your hands. Pinch one side of each ball into a small peak for the duck's tail, and place on the prepared baking sheet.

Take the remaining half of yellow icing, divide in half again, then divide one portion into 12 equal pieces. Roll each piece into a ball, then gently press onto each duck's body at the opposite side to the tail – this is the head. Divide the remaining yellow icing into 24 pieces and press into small wing shapes. Press one wing on each side of each duck.

To make the beaks, divide the orange icing into 12 pieces and shape into pyramids. Press one triangle onto the front of each duck head and gently form into a beak shape. Leave to set for 2 hours. Paint eyes onto each duck with a skewer dipped into the black food colouring.

The next day, preheat the oven to 180°C (350°F) Gas 4.

Prepare and bake the vanilla cupcakes. Cool for 3–4 minutes in the pans, then remove to cool completely on a wire rack.

Prepare the meringue buttercream and tint pale blue using the food colouring. Spoon it into the prepared pastry/piping bag and pipe generous swirls on top of each cupcake.

Scatter the blue and white sugar pearls over the buttercream, then sit a rubber ducky on top just before serving.

COOKIE POPS

Here's a neat and simple idea – cookies on a stick! Make a cookie landscape for your party table or buy a block of foam from a florist, cover it in foil or vibrant tissue paper and push the lollipop/popsicle sticks into it.

1 quantity Basic Vanilla Cookies (see page 16)
1 quantity Royal Icing (see page 22)

TO DECORATE
assorted gel or paste food colouring
pastry/cookie cutters in the shapes of ducks, butterflies, etc.
baking sheets, lined with baking parchment
about 16 oven-proof lollipop/ popsicle sticks
small pastry/piping bags, fitted with a fine writing nozzle/tip, or make your own (see page 29)

Makes 12–16

Prepare the vanilla cookie dough and, using the cutters, stamp out shapes and arrange on the prepared baking sheets, allowing plenty of space between each one. Gather the dough scraps together, knead lightly, re-roll and stamp out more cookies until all the dough has been used up. Push a lollipop/popsicle stick into the bottom of each cookie so that it is completely covered in dough and sticks into the cookie by about 2 cm/ ³⁄₄ inch. Refrigerate the cookies for 20 minutes while you preheat the oven to 160°C (325°F) Gas 3.

Bake the cookies on the middle shelf of the preheated oven for about 12 minutes or until pale golden – you may need to swap the sheets around halfway through baking to ensure that the cookies brown evenly. Leave to cool on the sheets for about 5 minutes before transferring to a wire rack to cool completely.

Prepare the royal icing. Depending on the colour scheme and creatures you have chosen, and the number of cookie shapes you are using, you will need to divide the icing between smaller bowls and tint accordingly using food colourings.

Follow the instructions on page 22 to frost the cookies using the 'flooding' technique. Leave to set for at least three hours before serving.

FLOCK OF FLUFFY SHEEP

Every flock should have just one black sheep amongst all the snowy white lambs.
Make a batch of these adorable chocolate gingerbread cookies for Easter.

1 quantity Basic Chocolate
   Gingerbread (see page 18)
plain/all-purpose flour,
   for dusting
1 quantity Royal Icing (see page 22)

TO DECORATE
pink and black gel or paste
   food colouring
sheep-shaped pastry/cookie cutters
baking sheets, lined with
   baking parchment
pastry/piping bags, or make
   your own (see page 29)

Makes 10–12

Prepare the chocolate gingerbread, stopping at the end of Step 3. Preheat the oven to 160°C (325°F) Gas 3.

Dust a clean surface with flour and roll the dough evenly to a thickness of 3 mm/$\frac{1}{8}$ inch. Use the cutters to stamp out as many cookies as possible from the dough, cutting each one as close as possible to the next one. Arrange the cookies on the prepared baking sheets. Gather the dough scraps together, knead lightly, re-roll and stamp out more cookies until all the dough has been used up. Bake the gingerbread in batches on the middle shelf of the preheated oven for 10–12 minutes or until firm and browned at the edges. Allow the cookies to cool completely on the baking sheets before icing.

Prepare the royal icing. Take out 1 tablespoon and tint pink using the food colouring. Cover and set aside. Take another 2 tablespoons of the icing and tint black for the one black sheep of the flock. Cover and set aside. Put the remaining white icing in one of the pastry/piping bags and pipe outlines around the edges of all but one of the sheep. (See page 22 for instructions on flooding.) Leave to set for at least 10 minutes.

Flood the insides of the outlines with white icing. Leave to set for at least 20 minutes.

Use the black icing to make legs, eyes and a nose on each sheep. Thicken the remaining white icing slightly by beating it vigorously for a minute or by adding more icing/confectioners' sugar. Pipe woolly squiggles over the body of the sheep and, using the tip of a knife or a teaspoon, give each sheep pink ears.

Make the black sheep using the method above and allow to dry completely before serving.

FARMYARD SUGAR MICE

What farm is complete without a few mice scurrying about? Make these at least one day before serving, to give them plenty of time to dry out. The recipe makes enough for a large family of mice - one for each of your family and friends.

1 egg white
1 teaspoon lemon juice
400–500 g/3–3¹/₂ cups icing/
   confectioners' sugar, sifted
pink gel or paste food colouring
small chocolate sprinkles
kitchen twine
cocktail stick/toothpick
baking sheet, lined with
   baking parchment

Makes 12

Put the egg white in a large bowl and whisk with a balloon whisk until foamy. Stir in the lemon juice.

Gradually add the icing/confectioners' sugar and stir in with a wooden spoon until really stiff, like dough. It might be easier to dust the work surface with icing/confectioners' sugar and knead the sugar into the mixture until you get the right consistency.

Divide the mixture in two. Add a dot pink food colouring to one half and knead it until all the colour is evenly mixed in. Add a tiny bit more colouring if you want a stronger colour.

Break off walnut-sized pieces of mixture and roll into a rounded cone shape and flatten one side so that each mouse can sit on a surface without wobbling over. Pinch little ears on top of the narrow end. Squeeze the narrow end into a nose. Press a chocolate sprinkle into the face below the ears to make the eyes. Cut a length of twine about 4 cm/1¹/₂ inches long and push it into the round end of the mouse to make the tail.

Use a cocktail stick/toothpick to dab a tiny amount of pink food colouring on the nose. Put the mouse on the prepared baking sheet.

Repeat with the remaining mixture and leave the mice to dry out for at least 12 hours.

PERFECT *Pets*

MUNGO THE DOG

Dogs are a beloved part of many families, so why not share the love by creating one for the centrepiece of your party. You need only one cupcake here – any remaining can be frozen for another time or decorated for extra cake servings!

1 quantity Large Basic Vanilla Cake
   mixture (see page 11)
1 quantity Vanilla Buttercream
   (see page 20)

TO DECORATE
200 g/7 oz. desiccated/
   dried shredded coconut
4 plain, shop-bought mini
   Swiss/jelly rolls
red gel or paste food colouring
silver sugar pearls
12 mini chocolate drops
2 white chocolate buttons
black writing icing
2 chocolate-coated wafers
1.2-litre/5-cup and 275-ml/1¼-cup
   pudding basins, greased with
   sunflower oil and dusted with flour
12-hole mini cupcake pan, lined
   with 8 mini cupcake cases
cocktail sticks/toothpicks
piping bag, fitted with a star-shaped
   nozzle/tip, or make your own
   (see page 29)

Serves 12

Preheat the oven to 180°C (350°F) Gas 4.

Make the vanilla cake mixture and spoon into the prepared basins until they are two-thirds full. Use the remaining mixture to fill the cupcakes cases, allowing roughly 1½–2 teaspoons of mixture per cupcake. Bake all the cakes in the middle of the preheated oven until an inserted skewer comes out clean – 10–15 minutes for the mini cupcakes, 30 minutes for the smaller basin and 40–45 minutes for the larger one. Cool for 10 minutes in the basins/pans, then remove to cool completely on a wire rack.

Put the desiccated/dried shredded coconut in a dry frying pan/skillet and toast until lightly golden, tossing frequently to stop it burning. Set aside to cool while you start on the cake.

If necessary, trim the tops of the cakes to make them level. Put the larger one, flat-side down, on a large plate. Take the smaller cake and put it, flat-side down, on a board. Trim a little off two sides to make a snout shape at the front of what will be the head. Arrange on top of the body, flat-side down, and slightly forwards. Secure with cocktail sticks/toothpicks. Peel the cupcake case off the mini cupcake and attach the cupcake to the snout with cocktail sticks/toothpicks. Arrange the mini rolls – two upright in front and two laying flat at the back – to make the legs.

Reserve 3–4 tablespoons of the buttercream in a small bowl. Coat the whole dog with the remaining buttercream, spreading evenly with a palette knife/metal spatula. Scatter the toasted coconut over the buttercream and press lightly to stick.

For the collar, tint the reserved buttercream red with the red food colouring and use to fill the pastry/piping bag. Pipe rosettes around the neck of the dog and decorate with silver sugar pearls.

For the claws, position mini chocolate drops at the front of each leg. For eyes, position white chocolate buttons on the head. Pipe a nose and mouth on the snout using black writing icing. Finally, push the chocolate-coated wafers into the top of the head for the ears.

MARMALADE CAT

As cute as any ginger cat, this cake is perfect for the novice baker, or baking with
a younger child, as it requires only two round cake pans and no tricky assembly.
You could also use brown or black tones to make a tabby or grey cat instead,
or you could frost the cake with Chocolate Fudge Frosting (see page 21).

1 quantity Medium Basic Vanilla
   Cake mixture (see page 11)
1 quantity Large Basic Vanilla Cake
   mixture (see page 11)
1 quantity Vanilla Buttercream
   (see page 20)

TO DECORATE
orange gel or paste food colouring
2 green soft fruit sweets/candies
   or similar
1 small black liquorice sweet/candy
1 long black liquorice strip/
   shoelace
black writing icing
*18-cm/7-inch and 23-cm/9-inch
   round cake pans, greased
   and lined with baking parchment
small pastry/piping bag, fitted with
   a fine writing nozzle/tip, or make
   your own (see page 29)*

Serves 12–14

Preheat the oven to 180°C (350°F) Gas 4.

Make the vanilla cake mixtures separately and spoon the medium quantity
into the smaller pan and the large quantity into the larger pan. Bake on
the middle shelf of the preheated oven until an inserted skewer comes
out clean – about 30 minutes for the smaller pan and 35–40 minutes for
the larger pan. Cool for 10 minutes in the pans, then remove to cool
completely on a wire rack.

Reserve 4–5 tablespoons of the buttercream in a small bowl. Tint the
remaining buttercream orange with the orange food colouring.

If necessary, trim the tops of the cakes to make them level, and the
same height.

Cut about one-third off the top of the larger cake, in a leaf shape, for the
smaller cake to fit into the space. Cut the removed leaf shape in half to
make two triangles and position at the top of the smaller cake for ears.
Secure all pieces in place with a little orange buttercream.

Coat the cat with the remaining orange buttercream, spreading evenly
with a palette knife/metal spatula. Carefully spread the reserved plain
buttercream to make a tummy shape and insides of the ears.

Position the soft fruit sweets/candies on the cat's face for the eyes. Slice
the liquorice sweet/candy into thin slices to make the nose and position
the liquorice strip/shoelace for the tail and the mouth. Use black writing
icing to make the whiskers and pupils in the eyes.

BUNNY RABBIT

This fluffy rabbit is coated with meringue frosting 'fur', but you could use the Vanilla Buttercream (see page 20) coloured to your desired shade. For the bunny's tail you need only one cupcake, so freeze the leftovers or turn them into flowers, and place them around the bunny.

1 quantity Extra Large Basic
   Vanilla Cake mixture (page 11)
1 quantity Small Basic Vanilla Cake
   mixture (page 11)
1 quantity Meringue Frosting
   (page 21)

TO DECORATE
pink gel or paste food colouring
2 Jelly Beans or brown candy-
   coated chocolate drops
black writing icing
33 x 23 x 6-cm/13 x 9 x 2½-inch
*   cake pan, greased and lined*
*   with baking parchment*
6-hole muffin pan, lined with
*   cupcake cases*
paper template of a rabbit the
*   same size as the cake pan (draw*
*   freehand and cut out with scissors*
*   or search online for 2D rabbit*
*   pictures to print and cut out)*

Serves 12

Preheat the oven to 180°C (350°F) Gas 4.

Make the vanilla cake mixtures separately and spoon the extra large into the prepared cake pan and divide the small between the cupcake cases. Bake on the middle shelf of the preheated oven until an inserted skewer comes out clean – 40 minutes for the cake and 20–25 minutes for the cupcakes. Cool for 10 minutes in the pans, then remove to cool completely on a wire rack.

When you are ready to assemble the cake, take your rabbit template, lay on top of the cake and, using a small, sharp knife, carefully cut around the paper template. Arrange your rabbit on a large platter.

Take 3–4 tablespoons of the meringue frosting for the ears and tail and set aside in a small bowl. Completely coat the top and sides of the rabbit with the plain meringue frosting, peaking the meringue with the back of a spoon so that it looks like fur.

Tint the reserved meringue frosting pale pink with the pink food colouring. Peel the cupcake case off one cupcake and coat the cupcake in pink frosting. Fill in the insides of the ears with pink frosting too. Position the flat side of the cupcake on top of the rabbit for a fluffy tail.

Position the Jelly Beans or chocolate drops on the rabbit's face to make an eye and the nose. Using the writing icing, draw whiskers on the face. Leave aside for about 1 hour to set slightly before serving.

Calling all pug-lovers! But be warned, this easy-to-make (and easy-to-love) cake may steal the limelight with its adorable puppy dog eyes.

ADORABLE PUG

1 quantity Large Basic Vanilla
or Chocolate Cake mixture
(see page 11) baked in two
23-cm/9-inch greased and lined
cake pans for 35–40 minutes,
until an inserted skewer comes
out clean, then cooled
1 quantity Vanilla Buttercream
(see page 20)

TO DECORATE
brown gel or paste food colouring
icing/confectioners' sugar,
for dusting
250 g/9 oz. dark brown or
chocolate fondant
10 g/$\frac{1}{3}$ oz. pink fondant icing
60 g/2 oz. black fondant icing
50 g/1$\frac{3}{4}$ oz. white fondant icing
4 white sugar pearls
paper straw
thin paintbrush
6-cm/2$\frac{1}{2}$-inch round
pastry/cookie cutter
5-cm/2-inch round
pastry/cookie cutter

Serves 24

Start by assembling the cakes. If necessary, trim the tops of the cakes to make them level. Sandwich together using 200 g/7 oz. of the buttercream – the bottom side of the top cake should be facing up. Place on a serving plate and crumb-coat (see page 27) the cake using 300 g/10$\frac{1}{2}$ oz. of the buttercream. Chill for 15 minutes.

Place the remaining buttercream in a bowl and tint it light brown. Use to coat the cake in a second layer of buttercream. Smooth and remove the excess buttercream with a palette knife/metal spatula.

For the snout, dust a surface and roll out the dark brown or chocolate fondant icing to 3 mm/$\frac{1}{8}$ inch thick. Cut out a slightly rounded triangle, with an approximate 12 cm/4$\frac{3}{4}$ inch long base and 8 cm/3$\frac{1}{4}$ inch long sides. Use the edge of the cake baking pan as a guide to get a rounded base. Place on top of the cake leaving a 5-mm/$\frac{1}{4}$-inch border from the edge of the cake. With a sharp knife, mark a wave shape for the mouth. Make indentations in the cheeks with the end of the straw.

For the darker fur behind the eyes, cut two large tear-drop shapes – 10 cm/4 inches in length and 7.5 cm/3 inches across at the widest point – from some of the remaining brown or chocolate fondant.

Next, the ears. Cut two slightly rounded triangles from the remaining brown or chocolate fondant, each with an approximate 11 cm/4$\frac{1}{4}$ inch long base and 8 cm/3$\frac{1}{4}$ inch long sides. Position by sticking the longest side to the base edge of the cake and bend the top tips of the triangle over the top of the cake so they just touch the tear-drop shapes.

To make the tongue, roll the pink icing into a smooth egg-shape, then flatten slightly. Make an indentation with the side of the paintbrush to the centre. Brush the back with a little water, then position in the middle of the mouth.

For the nose, roll 15 g/$\frac{1}{2}$ oz. of the black icing into an oval-shape and flatten slightly. Use the end of the thin paintbrush to make 'hook-shapes' for nostrils. Brush the back with a little water, then position.

Finally, create the eyes. Dust a surface and roll out the white icing to 2mm/$\frac{1}{16}$ inch thick. Use the larger cutter to cut out two circles. Repeat with the black icing using the smaller cutter. Brush one side of the white circles with a little water and stick to the dark fur. Repeat for the black circles and position on top of the white icing. Make two indentations in each eye with the paintbrush end. Brush each indentation with a little water and use to stick a white sugar pearl in each.

PERFECT PET CUPCAKES

These funny cupcakes look tricky but are actually very simple to make. The only fancy equipment you'll need is a couple of pastry/piping bags, nozzles/tips and a steady hand. Try different tones for their 'fur' to create an animal gathering of all different shades.

1 quantity Large Basic Vanilla Cake mixture (see page 11)
1 quantity Vanilla Buttercream (see page 20)

TO DECORATE
brown and black gel or paste food colouring
2 small liquorice sweets/candies
12 candy-coated chocolate drops
black writing icing
3 pastry/piping bags, fitted with star-shaped nozzles/tips, or make your own (see page 29)
12-hole muffin pan, lined with paper cupcake cases
12-hole mini muffin pan, lined with mini paper cupcake cases

Makes 12

Preheat the oven to 180°C (350°F) Gas 4.

Make the vanilla cake mixture and use to fill each cupcake case with a tablespoon measure, and the mini cases with a teaspoon measure. Bake on the middle shelf of the preheated oven – 20–25 minutes for the cupcakes, 10–15 minutes for the mini cupcakes – until a skewer inserted into the middle of the cakes comes out clean. Leave to cool in the pans for 10 minutes, then transfer to a wire rack to cool completely.

Divide the buttercream between three bowls and tint one brown and one grey with the brown and black food colouring. Leave the third bowl of buttercream plain.

Fill the pastry/piping bags each with a different buttercream. Pipe lines of buttercream on top of the cupcakes, from the outside to the centre in a slight dome. Coat four of the cupcakes with brown buttercream, four with grey and four with plain. Repeat with the mini cupcakes, making pointed buttercream ears at the top of each cake.

Cut the liquorice into tiny pieces for noses and position one on each mini cupcake. Cut the chocolate drops in half and position on the ears. Using the black writing icing, pipe eyes and whiskers onto each mini cupcake. Position the mini cupcakes on top of the cupcakes and gently push together until they are firmly stuck in place.

DOG KENNEL

Give a dog a home with this fabulous chocolate kennel. To get ahead,
make the cake mixture and cookie dough the day before serving.

**250 g/2 sticks unsalted butter,
softened**

**250 g/1¼ cups caster/
superfine sugar**

4 eggs, beaten

1 teaspoon pure vanilla extract

250 g/2 cups plain/all-purpose flour

4 teaspoons baking powder

**3–4 tablespoons milk, at room
temperature**

**1 quantity Vanilla Buttercream
(see page 20)**

200 g/7 oz. milk chocolate

25 g/1 oz. white chocolate

**200–250 g/7–9 oz. milk chocolate
buttons**

50 g/2 oz. white chocolate chips

DOGS

plain/all-purpose flour, for dusting

**1 quantity Gingerbread Cookies
(see page 19)**

1 quantity Royal Icing (see page 22)

**assorted gel or paste food
colouring, to match your
breeds of dog!**

*23 x 33 x 6-cm/9 x 13 x 2½-inch
baking pan, lined with baking
parchment*

*assorted dog-shaped
pastry/cookie cutters*

*2 baking sheets, lined with
baking parchment*

*small pastry/piping bag, fitted with
a fine writing nozzle/tip, or make
your own (see page 15)*

Preheat the oven to 180°C (350°F) Gas 4.

Cream together the butter and sugar until light and creamy. Gradually add
the beaten eggs, mixing well between each addition and scraping down the
side of the mixing bowl from time to time. Add the vanilla extract. Sift together
the flour and baking powder and add to the mixture in two batches. Stir in the
milk. Mix until smooth, then spoon into the prepared baking pan and spread
level with a palette knife/metal spatula.

Bake on the middle shelf of the preheated oven for 35–40 minutes until an
inserted skewer comes out clean. Cool for 5 minutes in the pans, then remove
to cool completely on a wire rack. Once cold, wrap in clingfilm/plastic wrap
until you are ready to assemble the dog kennel. Leave the oven on to bake
the dog cookies.

Dust a clean surface and roll the gingerbread cookie dough 3 mm/⅛ inch
thick. Using the cutters, stamp out dog shapes and carefully arrange them
on the prepared baking sheets allowing plenty of space between each one.
Gather the dough scraps together, knead lightly, re-roll and stamp out more
cookies until all the dough has been used up. Bake the cookies on the middle
shelf of the preheated oven for 10–12 minutes or until the edges are just
starting to brown – you may need to swap the sheets around halfway through
baking to ensure that the cookies brown evenly. Leave to cool on the sheets
for about 5 minutes before transferring to a wire rack to cool completely.

Divide the royal icing between however many bowls you need for the colours
you're using and tint each a different colour using the food colouring. Fill the
pastry/piping bag with the colour you want to start with. Pipe borders around
the cookies. Flood (see page 22) the area inside the borders with icing,
spreading it carefully up to the edges with a mini palette knife/metal spatula
or small knife. Leave it to dry and harden slightly, then decorate or
accessorize as you like!

When you are ready to assemble the cake, cut it into quarters and place one
quarter on a serving platter. Sandwich the pieces together using the vanilla

Continued on page 104

Serves 8–10

(1)

(2)

buttercream, spreading evenly with a palette knife/metal spatula. Repeat so that you have four layers of cake and three layers of buttercream. Using a long knife, cut into the long sides to make a roof shape. Coat the whole cake with buttercream and leave to cool.

Make the chocolate panels as described to the right. At the same time, make a door shape out of the white chocolate. Cut the panels to fit the walls of the dog kennel (vertically for the short sides and horizontally for the long). Stick them to the buttercream. Attach the door with a little buttercream. Tile the roof with the milk chocolate buttons, filling in the gaps with the white chocolate chips. Arrange the dogs in front of the kennel and serve.

TO MAKE THE CHOCOLATE PANELS

Put the milk chocolate, chopped, in a heatproof bowl set over a pan of barely simmering water. Stir until thoroughly smooth and melted.

Pour the melted chocolate onto a baking sheet lined with baking parchment. Spread into a thin layer using a palette knife/metal spatula and leave aside until completely set.

Using a large, sharp knife, trim the edges of the chocolate to make an even rectangle. Cut into strips about 2 cm/^{3}/$_4$ inch wide. (1)

Trim the strips so that they are just a little taller than the frosted cake. (2)

Repeat the steps above with white chocolate, chopped, for the door.

WITCHES' CATS AND HATS

Purrrfect for Halloween or any other witchy-themed occasion. Look for different shapes of cat cutters and edible Halloween sprinkles in green, orange and black in cake-decorating stores or online suppliers.

**Basic Spiced or Chocolate
   Gingerbread (see page 18)**

TO DECORATE
**plain/all-purpose flour,
   for dusting**
1 quantity Royal Icing (see page 22)
**green and black gel or paste food
   colouring**
orange and black sprinkles
orange and green sanding sugar
*cat and witches'-hat
   pastry/cookie cutters*
*baking sheets, lined with
   baking parchment*
*2 small pastry/piping bags, fitted with
   a fine writing nozzle/tip, or make
   your own (see page 29)*

Makes 10–12

First, prepare the gingerbread according to the recipe on page 18, stopping at the end of Step 3. Preheat the oven to 170°C (325°F) Gas 3.

Dust a clean surface and roll the gingerbread 3 mm/$1/8$ inch thick. Using the cutters, stamp out cat and hat shapes and carefully arrange them on the prepared baking sheets allowing plenty of space between each one. Gather the dough scraps together, knead lightly, re-roll and stamp out more cookies until all the dough has been used up. Bake the gingerbread in batches on the middle shelf of the preheated oven for 10–12 minutes or until the edges are just starting to brown. Leave to cool on the sheets for about 5 minutes before transferring to a wire rack to cool completely.

Prepare the royal icing. Leave two teaspoons of the icing in the mixing bowl and cover and set aside. Put 3–4 tablespoons in a small bowl and tint this green using the food colouring. Cover and set aside. In a third bowl tint the remaining icing black.

Fill the pastry/piping bag with the black icing and pipe a fine line around the edge of each cookie. (See page 22 for instructions on flooding.) Leave to dry for at least 10 minutes. Flood the insides of the outlines with black icing. Tip the orange and black sprinkles into a saucer and dip the bottom edge of each hat in the sprinkles. Leave to dry for 20 minutes.

Fill another pastry/piping bag with the reserved green icing and pipe a green band around each hat and a collar on each cat. Carefully sprinkle orange and green sanding sugar on the hat bands. Give each cat a set of white eyes, using the reserved white icing and dot with a little black icing. Leave to dry completely before serving.

EASTER EGGS AND BUNNIES

Create a pretty Easter theme with assorted Easter-related cookie cutters. If you can't find bunny- or egg-shaped cutters, make paper templates, lay over the cookie dough and carefully cut out using a small, sharp knife. These Easter bunnies are made with a large cutter, but feel free to use a smaller breed!

1 quantity Basic Vanilla Cookies or Gingerbread Cookies (see pages 16 and 19)

TO DECORATE
plain/all-purpose flour, for dusting
2 quantities Royal Icing (see page 22)
brown, pink, blue, lilac and black gel or paste food colouring
white nonpareils or sugar strands
Easter egg-shaped pastry/cookie cutters
bunny rabbit-shaped pastry/cookie cutter
2 baking sheets, lined with baking parchment
small pastry/piping bag, fitted with a fine writing nozzle/tip, or make your own (see page 29)
narrow gingham ribbon (optional)

Makes 10–12

First, prepare the basic vanilla cookie or gingerbread cookie dough. Dust a clean work surface and roll to 3 mm/⅛ inch thick. Using the cookie cutters, stamp out egg and bunny shapes and carefully arrange them on the prepared baking sheets, allowing plenty of space between each one. Gather the dough scraps together, knead lightly, re-roll and stamp out more cookies until all the dough has been used up. Chill for 15 minutes.

Preheat the oven to 180°C (350°F) Gas 4.

Bake the cookies on the middle shelf of the preheated oven for about 12 minutes, until firm or starting to brown – you may need to swap the sheets around halfway through baking to ensure that the cookies brown evenly. Leave to cool on the sheets for about 5 minutes before transferring to a wire rack to cool completely.

Divide the royal icing between six bowls. Tint each one a different colour using the food colouring. You will only need a tiny amount of the black icing. Leave the last bowl of icing plain.

Fill the pastry/piping bag with whichever colour you want to start with and pipe a fine line around the egg-shaped cookies. (See page 22 for instructions on flooding.) Flood the area inside the borders with icing: once you have made a neat border, you can spoon icing within the borders and spread it carefully up to the edges with a mini palette knife/metal spatula or small knife. Leave to dry and harden slightly before going any further. Pipe in the rest of the design: draw lines, squiggles and dots over each egg. Leave to dry completely.

Repeat the same technique for icing the bunnies using brown icing. Pipe in noses, mouths and eyes with the black icing. Finish off each rabbit with a fluffy tail: pipe a large blob of white icing in the correct position and scatter with the nonpareils or sugar strands.

Once the icing has completely set, tie a length of gingham ribbon around the neck of each bunny and serve alongside the eggs.

GIVE A DOG A BONE

Dog-shaped cookie cutters are available in just about every shape and breed imaginable so you can really go to town and make a whole host of furry friends!

1 quantity Basic Spiced
　　Gingerbread (see page 18)

TO DECORATE
plain/all-purpose flour,
　　for dusting
1 quantity Royal Icing (see page 22)
brown, black, blue and red gel or
　　paste food colouring
silver sugar pearls
bone-shaped pastry/cookie cutter
assorted dog-shaped pastry/
　　cookie cutters
baking sheets, lined with
　　baking parchment
small pastry/piping bag, fitted with
　　a fine writing nozzle/tip, or make
　　your own (see page 29)

Makes 10-12

Prepare the basic spiced gingerbread according to the recipe on page 18, stopping at the end of Step 3. Preheat the oven to 160°C (325°F) Gas 3.

Dust a clean surface and roll the gingerbread 3 mm/⅛ inch thick. Using the cutters, stamp out dog shapes and carefully arrange them on the prepared baking sheets allowing plenty of space between each one. Gather the dough scraps together, knead lightly, re-roll and stamp out more cookies until all the dough has been used up. Bake the gingerbread in batches on the middle shelf of the preheated oven for 10–12 minutes or until the edges are just starting to brown. Leave to cool on the sheets for about 5 minutes before transferring to a wire rack to cool completely.

Prepare the royal icing and leave one half of the icing in the mixing bowl and divide the remaining icing between two small bowls. Using the food colouring, tint one bowl brown and one black. Take out one tablespoon of icing from the white icing and, in a separate bowl, tint this blue or red for the collars. Cover and set aside.

Fill the pastry/piping bag with two tablespoons of the white icing and pipe a border around the edge of each bone and white-coloured dog. (See page 23 for instructions on flooding.) Repeat with the brown and black icings for any brown- or black-coloured dogs. Leave to dry for at least 10 minutes, then flood the insides of the outlines with the corresponding icing. If your dogs have patches of colour, you need to do this before the icing sets. Add patches of brown and black to make white terriers. Leave to dry for 20 minutes.

Finally, pipe eyes and blue or red collars onto each dog. Decorate each collar with silver sugar pearls. Leave to dry completely before serving.

Garden
CRITTERS

SUMMER GARDEN CAKE

200 g/7 oz. white flower
   modelling paste
assorted gel or paste food
   colouring
icing/confectioners' sugar,
   for dusting
1 quantity Royal Icing (see page 22)
1 quantity Vanilla Cake mixture
   (see page 12)
1 quantity Meringue Buttercream
   (see page 21)
3 tablespoons good lemon curd,
   strawberry jam/jelly or
   raspberry jam/jelly
*assorted butterfly-
   and flower-shaped
   pastry/cookie cutters*
*3 x 20-cm/8-inch round cake
   pans, greased and lined
   with baking parchment*
*pastry/piping bags, or make
   your own (see page 29)*

Serves 12

This cake with its garden of fluttering butterflies would be just the ticket for a birthday party, a baby shower or just for a special spring-time treat. To get ahead, you will need to prepare the butterflies and flowers at least 24 hours in advance.

Make the butterflies and flowers at least 24 hours before you bake the cake. See page 26 for instructions on how to make them. Use the modelling paste tinted in whichever colours you like using food colourings, and make the butterflies and flowers in varying sizes and colours.

Once the basic butterfly and flower shapes have dried sufficiently, decorate them with royal icing. Make up small batches of icing in various shades to suit the colour palette you have chosen and spoon them into the pastry/piping bags. Snip the ends to fine points and pipe decorative patterns over the butterflies and flowers. Leave to dry for at least a couple of hours before using to decorate the finished cake.

When you are ready to make the cake, preheat the oven to 180°C (350°F) Gas 4.

Prepare the vanilla cake mixture and divide the mixture evenly between the prepared pans. Bake the cakes on the middle shelf of the preheated oven for about 25 minutes until an inserted skewer comes out clean. Cool for 10 minutes in the pans, then remove to cool completely on a wire rack.

Meanwhile, use a little food colouring of your choice to tint the meringue buttercream – stir it in gradually until you get the pale shade you like.

Assemble the cake. If necessary, trim the tops of the cakes to make them level. Place one of the cake layers on a serving dish. Sandwich together using 2–3 tablespoons of meringue buttercream and a half the lemon curd – layering carefully so they don't blend – between each cake. The bottom side of the top cake should be facing up. Spread the remaining meringue buttercream evenly over the top and side of the cake using a palette knife/metal spatula. Chill for 30 minutes.

When you are ready to serve the cake, decorate with the butterflies and flowers, pressing them gently into the buttercream on the top of the cake, and then around to one side.

LUCY LADYBUG

One of the most cheerful-looking garden critters, this ladybug's body should be tinted in the brightest red you can find. Pipe cleaners are available in most craft shops and will make great antennae for all manner of creatures.

1 quantity Large Basic Vanilla Cake mixture (see page 11)
1 quantity Small Basic Vanilla Cake mixture (see page 11)
1 quantity Vanilla Buttercream (see page 20)

TO DECORATE
red and black gel or paste food colouring
long liquorice strip/shoelace
giant milk chocolate buttons
2 yellow Smarties/candy-coated chocolates

2-litre/2-quart/8-cup round Pyrex bowl, greased with sunflower oil and dusted with flour
6-hole muffin pan, lined with cupcake cases
2 red pipe cleaners

Serves 8–10

Preheat the oven to 180°C (350°F) Gas 4.

Make the vanilla cake mixtures separately and spoon the large quantity into the prepared bowl and divide the small quantity between the cupcake cases. Bake just under the middle shelf of the preheated oven until an inserted skewer comes out clean – 40–45 minutes for the cake and 20–25 minutes for the cupcakes. Cool for 10 minutes in the bowl and pan, then remove to cool completely on a wire rack.

Put three-quarters of the buttercream in a bowl and tint it bright red with the red food colouring. Tint the remaining buttercream black.

If necessary, trim the bottom of the domed cake to make it level. Place the cake, flat-side down, on a serving plate and coat with the red buttercream, spreading evenly with a palette knife/metal spatula. Stick the liquorice strip/shoelace along the middle of the body and arrange the chocolate buttons on either side.

Peel the cupcake case off one cupcake (freeze the rest of the cupcakes for another time) and level off the domed top. Coat the cupcake with the black buttercream, spreading evenly with a palette knife/metal spatula, and place it upside-down on the plate against the ladybug's body, at one end of the liquorice strip/shoelace.

Position the yellow Smarties/candy-coated chocolates on the head for the eyes and push the pipe cleaners into the top for the antennae.

CURLY CATERPILLAR

Popular with younger children, this cake is a doddle to make - everything is done the day of the party and the decorating is very simple.

1 quantity Extra Large Basic Vanilla Cake mixture (see page 11)

1 quantity Small Basic Vanilla Cake mixture (see page 11)

1 quantity Vanilla Buttercream (see page 20)

TO DECORATE

yellow, red, green, mauve and blue gel or paste food colouring

liquorice strips/shoelaces

16 jelly beans

2 Smarties/candy-coated chocolates

assorted coloured writing icing

1-litre/4-cup, 650-ml/2⅓-cup and 2 x 350-ml/1½-cup round Pyrex bowls, greased and dusted with flour

6-hole muffin pan, lined with cupcake cases

2 green pipe cleaners

Serves 10–12

Preheat the oven to 180°C (350°F) Gas 4.

Make the vanilla cake mixtures separately and divide the extra large quantity between the prepared bowls and the small quantity between the cupcake cases. Bake just under the middle shelf of the preheated oven until an inserted skewer comes out clean – 45–55 minutes for the larger bowls, 30–35 minutes for the smaller bowls and 20–25 minutes for the cupcakes. Cool for 10 minutes in the pans, then remove to cool completely on a wire rack. If necessary, trim the bottom of the domed cake to make it level.

Divide the buttercream between five bowls and tint each one a different colour with the food colourings and set aside. Bear in mind that the quantity of buttercream needed for each cake will differ slightly depending on the cake sizes.

Coat each cake a with different colour of buttercream, spreading evenly with a palette knife/metal spatula.

Peel the cupcake case off one cupcake (freeze the rest of the cupcakes for another time). Coat the cupcake with the fifth colour of buttercream. Arrange all the cakes on a serving board in a curly caterpillar shape and in decreasing size of cake.

Cut the liquorice strip/shoelace into 17 x 5-cm/2-inch lengths and position in pairs on either side of each cake as legs. Stick the last length of liquorice to the largest cake at the front of the caterpillar as a mouth. Position the jelly beans on the ends of the legs as feet. Stick the Smarties/candy-coated chocolates above the mouth for the eyes and push the pipe cleaners into the top for the antennae.

Use the writing icing to spell out the child's name along one side of the caterpillar and to add more decoration, if desired.

BUZZING BEEHIVE

Look out for insect-shaped candies or pretty foil-covered chocolate critters in candy shops and gift shops. Complete the theme with some flowery cupcakes.

2 quantities Large Basic Vanilla Cake mixture (see page 11)
1 quantity Vanilla Buttercream (see page 14)

TO DECORATE
yellow gel or paste food colouring
black writing icing
foil-covered chocolate bees
23-cm/9-inch and 18-cm/7-inch cake pans, greased and lined with baking parchment
6-hole muffin pan, lined with cupcake cases

Serves 12

Preheat the oven to 180°C (350°F) Gas 4.

Make the vanilla cake mixtures separately and spoon one quantity into the larger prepared cake pan and divide the other quantity between the smaller pan and the cupcake cases. Bake on the middle shelf of the preheated oven until an inserted skewer comes out clean – 40 minutes for the larger pan, 25 minutes for the smaller pan and 20–25 minutes for the cupcakes. Cool for 10 minutes in the pans, then remove to cool completely on a wire rack.

Tint the buttercream pale yellow with the yellow food colouring and set aside.

Trim the tops of the cakes to make level, if necessary. Place the large cake on a serving plate, take the smaller cake and sandwich together using a little buttercream – the bottom side of the top cake should be facing up.

Peel the cupcake case off one cupcake (freeze the rest of the cupcakes for another time). Position the cupcake, flat-side down, on top of the cake. Stick in place with a little more of the buttercream.

Coat the beehive with the remaining buttercream, spreading evenly with a palette knife/metal spatula. Use the black writing icing to pipe a geometric pattern over the beehive. Finally, arrange the chocolate bees around the cake to serve.

CREEPY HALLOWEEN CAKE

The white frosting on this cake hides a spooky surprise underneath. The cake mixture is divided in two and tinted orange and green, then marbled together before baking. You could also decorate the cake with more spooky toy spiders.

1 quantity Vanilla Cake mixture
   (see page 12)
orange and green gel or paste
   food colouring
1 quantity Meringue Buttercream
   (see page 21)

TO DECORATE
black gel or paste food colouring
green and/or orange sanding sugar
2 tablespoons black sprinkles/
   nonpareils or sanding sugar
½ quantity Royal Icing (see page 22)
thin liquorice strips/shoelaces
mini orange or yellow candy-coated
   chocolates
*2 x 20-cm/8-inch round cake pans,
   greased and lined with
   baking parchment*
*15-cm/6-inch round cake pan,
   greased and lined with
   baking parchment*
*muffin pan, lined with
   2–3 cupcake cases*
*pastry/piping bag, or make
   your own (see page 29)*

Serves 8–10

Preheat the oven to 180°C (350°F) Gas 4.

Prepare the vanilla cake mixture and divide evenly between two bowls. Using the food colourings, tint one bowl bright orange and the other bright green. Using a tablespoon, drop alternate spoonfuls of the two mixtures into the prepared cake pans, filling them halfway up. Fill the cupcake cases with alternate tablespoons of the cake mixtures, too. Drag a round-bladed knife through each mixture to create a marbled effect. Repeat this process with the cupcakes in the muffin pan.

Bake everything on the middle shelves of the preheated oven for about 20–35 minutes, depending on their size, until an inserted skewer comes out clean. Cool for 3–4 minutes in the pans, then remove to cool completely on a wire rack.

Tint four tablespoons of the meringue buttercream black using the food colouring and set aside.

Assemble the cake. If necessary, trim the tops of the cakes to make them level. Place one of the larger cakes on a serving dish. Take the other larger cake and sandwich together using a little of the plain buttercream. Take the smaller cake and repeat – the bottom side of the top cake should be facing up. Spread a thin layer of plain buttercream over the cake. Chill for 10 minutes. Coat the cake with another thin layer of untinted buttercream and sprinkle green and/or orange sanding sugar over it.

Peel the cupcake cases off the cupcakes and slice the cupcakes in half horizontally. Coat them with the black buttercream and scatter with the black sprinkles/nonpareils, or sanding sugar, evenly to coat.

Make up the royal icing and tint black using the food colouring. Spoon the black icing into the pastry/piping bag and snip the end to a fine point. Pipe spider's webs all over the cake.

Press short lengths of the liquorice into the sides of the cupcakes as spider's legs and give each spider two orange or yellow eyes with the Smarties/candy-coated chocolates. Arrange the spiders around the cake to serve.

PRICKLY HEDGEHOG

Don't be alarmed, this cute character isn't as prickly as he looks - the
chocolate matchstick spines are a delicious treat to eat alongside
the cake beneath it. You could even buy extra matchsticks and
make the extra cupcakes into baby hedgehogs!

**1 quantity Large Basic Vanilla
or Chocolate Cake mixture
(see page 11)**
**1 quantity Small Basic Vanilla
or Chocolate Cake mixture
(see page 11)**
**1 quantity Chocolate Fudge
Frosting (see page 21)**

TO DECORATE
chocolate sprinkles
**500 g/1 lb. 2 oz. chocolate
mint matchsticks**
3 chocolate drops
*2-litre/2-quart/8-cup round Pyrex
bowl, greased with sunflower
oil and dusted with flour*
*6-hole muffin pan, lined with
cupcake cases*

Serves 10

Preheat the oven to 180°C (350°F) Gas 4.

Make the vanilla cake mixtures separately and spoon the large into the
prepared bowl and divide the small between the cupcake cases. Bake
just under the middle shelf of the preheated oven until an inserted
skewer comes out clean – 1 hour for the cake and 20–25 minutes for
the cupcakes. Cool for 10 minutes in the bowl and pan, then remove
to cool completely on a wire rack.

If necessary, trim the bottom of the domed cake to make it level. Cut
the cake into three even horizontal layers. Sandwich together with
three tablespoons of chocolate fudge frosting between each layer.

Place the cake on a serving plate and coat it with most of the
remaining chocolate frosting (leaving enough to cover the cupcake),
spreading evenly with a palette knife/metal spatula.

Peel the cupcake case off one cupcake (freeze the rest of the
cupcakes for another time) and level off the domed top. Turn upside
down and coat the top and sides with the reserved chocolate frosting.
Scatter with the chocolate sprinkles and position on the plate next to
the larger cake for the head.

To make the spines, cut the matchsticks in half and push them
into the body of the hedgehog until it is totally covered. Push two
chocolate drops into the head for eyes, and one at the bottom for
the nose.

BELLA BUTTERFLY

Feel free to be as creative as you like with the patterns on the butterfly wings. Any leftover cake trimmings can either be used in a trifle or as a lunchbox treat.

2 quantities Large Basic Vanilla Cake mixture (see page 11)
1 quantity Vanilla Buttercream (see page 20)

TO DECORATE
brown and red gel or paste food colouring
black and red writing icing
2 short liquorice strips/shoelaces
6 sprinkle-coated chocolate buttons or similar
assorted sweets/candies and sprinkles
33 x 23 x 6-cm/13 x 9 x 2½-inch cake pan, greased and lined with baking parchment
pastry/piping bag, fitted with a star-shaped nozzle/tip, or make your own (see page 29)
A4-sized paper template of a butterfly (draw freehand and cut out with scissors or search online for 2D butterfly pictures to print and cut out)

Serves 12–14

Preheat the oven to 180°C (350°F) Gas 4.

Make one quantity of the large cake mixture and spoon into the prepared cake pan. Bake on the middle shelf of the preheated oven for 30 minutes until an inserted skewer comes out clean. Leave the oven on. Cool for 10 minutes in the pan, then remove to cool completely on a wire rack.

Clean the cake pan, then grease and line it again. Repeat the step above with the second quantity of cake mixture.

If necessary, trim the tops of the cakes to make them level. Lay the cakes side by side on a large platter.

When you are ready to assemble the cake, take your butterfly template, lay on top of the cake and, using a small, sharp knife, carefully cut around the paper template. Repeat with the second cake. Use the leftover bits of cake for a trifle, in lunchboxes or to snack on.

Set aside about 6 tablespoons of the buttercream in a small bowl. Tint the remaining buttercream brown with the brown food colouring and use to coat the top and sides of the butterfly, spreading evenly with a palette knife/metal spatula. Tint the reserved buttercream red and use to fill the pastry/piping bag. Pipe rosettes along the outer edges of the butterfly wings.

Pipe the outline of a body in the middle of the butterfly with the black writing icing and outline the wings with red writing icing. Push the liquorice strips/shoelaces into the top of the butterfly as antennae and decorate the wings with assorted sweets/candies and sprinkles.

LADYBUG CUPCAKES

These little ladybug cupcakes are a breeze to make and little hands
will love helping out with the assembling.

1 quantity Vanilla or Chocolate
   Cupcakes mixture
   (see page 14 or 15)
½ quantity Meringue Buttercream
   (see page 21)

TO DECORATE
400 g/14 oz. ready-to-roll
   fondant icing
red and black gel or paste
   food colouring
icing/confectioners' sugar,
   for dusting
*12-hole muffin pan, lined with
   cupcake cases*
*round pastry/cookie cutter, slightly
   wider than the widest part of
   the holes of the muffin pan*

Makes 12

Preheat the oven to 180°C (350°F) Gas 4.

Prepare and bake the vanilla or chocolate cupcakes as described on pages
14 or 15. Cool for 3–4 minutes in the pans, then remove to cool completely
on a wire rack.

Prepare the meringue buttercream and spread a level tablespoon of
buttercream smoothly over the top of each cupcake with a palette knife/
metal spatula.

Break off a small nugget of ready-to-roll fondant icing and wrap in clingfilm/
plastic wrap until ready to use.

Knead a few drop of the red colouring into two-thirds of the remaining icing.
Repeat to tint the remaining icing black and wrap in clingfilm/plastic wrap
and set aside.

Dust a clean work surface and roll out the reserved red icing to 2 mm/$\frac{1}{16}$ inch
thick. Use the cutter to stamp out 12 circles and lay one circle on top of each
cake. Gently smooth down into place to completely cover the buttercream.

Dust a clean work surface and roll out the reserved black icing to 2 mm/
$\frac{1}{16}$ inch thick. Use the cutter to stamp out six circles. Now stamp two
leaf-shaped halves from each disc using the cutter (reserve the trimmings).
These are for the ladybug's head. Brush a little water on one side of each
leaf shape and place on top of the red-covered cakes along one edge.

Using the blunt side of a knife, score a line down the middle of each ladybug
from the middle of the head to the tail-end. Roll the black icing trimmings into
little balls and gently flatten into even-sized pairs of circles. Brush with a little
water and stick the circles in a symmetrical pattern on either side of each
ladybug's back.

Using the reserved white icing, roll out 24 small balls and slightly flatten into
circles. Stick two on each ladybug's head for eyes. Finally, finish the eyes with
another small ball from the reserved black icing. Leave to set for at least an
hour before serving.

BUTTERFLY CUPCAKES

A step up from the more traditional butterffy cupcakes you used to make when you were little, these have painted sugar-paste wings to make them look ready for fflight! Once you have mastered the technique for making and painting the wings, you can let your imagination run wild with all different patterns.

1 quantity Buttermilk Cake mixture
    (see page 12)
1 quantity Meringue Buttercream
    (see page 21)

TO DECORATE
assorted coloured sprinkles

BUTTERFLIES
icing/confectioners' sugar,
    for dusting
250 g/9 oz. white sugar paste
1 quantity Royal Icing (see page 22)
pink, yellow and brown gel or paste
    food colouring
1–2 muffin pans, lined with
    cupcake cases
butterfly-shaped pastry/cookie cutter
small pastry/piping bag, fitted with
    a fine writing nozzle/tip, or make
    your own (see page 29)
wooden skewer or cocktail stick/
    toothpick

Makes 12–16

Preheat the oven to 180°C (350°F) Gas 4.

Divide the buttermilk cake mixture between the paper cupcake cases, filling them two-thirds full, and bake on the middle shelf of the preheated oven for 20 minutes until an inserted skewer comes out clean. Cool for 5 minutes in the pans, then remove to cool completely on a wire rack.

Spread the meringue buttercream over the tops of the cupcakes and then scatter over the sprinkles.

Get your butterfly cutter, pastry/piping bag and a wooden skewer or cocktail stick/toothpick ready to create the sugar-paste butterflies.

Refer to the step instructions on page 132 for making the sugar-paste butterflies. When the butterflies are completely dry, place matching pairs of wings on the cupcakes, pushing them at an angle into the buttercream topping.

HOW TO MAKE SUGAR PASTE BUTTERFLIES

Lightly dust a clean, dry work surface with icing/confectioners' sugar. Roll the sugar paste out to a thickness of no more than 3 mm/⅛ inch.

Using the butterfly-shaped cutter, stamp out the desired number of shapes. (1)

Cut each butterfly in half through the body to create 2 wings and set aside on baking parchment to dry out overnight. (2)

Divide the Royal Icing between three bowls. Tint one pink and one yellow using the food colourings. Tint them the shade of pink or yellow you like by very gradually adding more colouring. Leave the third bowl of icing white.

Pour 2–3 tablespoons of the white icing into your pastry/piping bag.

Working on one wing at a time, pipe a border around the wing. Flood the inner half of the wing, nearest the butterfly's body, with white icing (see page 22 for instructions on flooding) by spreading it to the inner edge with a mini palette knife/metal spatula or small knife.

Fill the other half of the wing with either pink or yellow icing, spreading to the outer edge and inwards to meet the white icing. (3)

Using the tip of the skewer, drag the coloured icing into the white to create a feathered effect. (4) Leave to dry. Repeat with the remaining wings.

Tint a small amount of the white icing brown and use to pipe a small line down the middle of each wing to create the body. (5)

Leave the wings to dry completely.

GARDEN CRITTERS

Watch out! Here's an invasion of edible bugs and critters that are a treat to decorate. Let loose with the pastry/piping bag and food colouring (within reason!) and design your own bright critters.

1 quantity Basic Vanilla Cookies (see page 16)
1 quantity Royal Icing (see page 22)

TO DECORATE
assorted gel or paste food colouring
critter-shaped pastry/cookie cutters (e.g. snail, ladybug, butterfly, caterpillar)
2 baking sheets, lined with baking parchment
small pastry/piping bag, fitted with a fine writing nozzle/tip, or make your own (see page 29)

Makes 12–18

Preheat the oven to 180°C (350°F) Gas 4.

You should have rolled out the basic vanilla cookie dough to of 3 mm/⅛ inch thick. Using the cutters, stamp out critter shapes and carefully arrange them on the prepared baking sheets allowing plenty of space between each one. Gather the dough scraps together, knead lightly, re-roll and stamp out more cookies until all the dough has been used up. Chill for 15 minutes. Bake the cookies in batches on the middle shelf of the preheated oven for 10–12 minutes or until the edges are just starting to brown. Leave to cool on the sheets for about 5 minutes before transferring to a wire rack to cool completely.

Divide the royal icing between the number of bowls you need for your colours of icing. Tint each one a different colour using the food colourings.

Fill the pastry/piping bag with whichever colour you want to start with and pipe borders around the cookies. Flood the area inside the borders with icing (see page 22 for instructions on flooding): once you have made a neat border, you can spoon icing within the borders and spread it carefully up to the edges with a mini palette knife/metal spatula or small knife.

Leave it to dry and harden slightly before you pipe your other lines or other features on top of the flooded icing. Leave to set before serving.

GINGERBREAD BIRDHOUSE

Gingerbread houses come in all shapes and sizes but this one has a special charm and quirkiness. You can go detailed as you like with the decorations, using homemade or store-bought, as you wish. As for the birds, the feathered friends pictured are very cute (available from craft supply stores) but you could make gingerbread birds (like the dogs on page 111) in a variety of shades and sprinkles.

2 quantities Basic Spiced
    Gingerbread (see page 18)

TO DECORATE
plain/all-purpose flour,
    for dusting
2 tablespoons strawberry
    or apricot jam/jelly
300 g/10 oz. ready-to-roll
    fondant icing
assorted gel or paste food
    colouring
400 g/2²/₃ cups royal icing
    sugar/mix
edible sugar mimosa balls
white Sugar-paste Daisies
    (see page 26)
butterfly-shaped candy sprinkles
assorted colours Smarties/
    candy-coated chocolates
baking parchment or tracing paper
    for making templates
2 or 3 large baking sheets,
    lined with baking parchment
small round pastry/cookie cutter
    to accommodate your
    decorative birds
heart-shaped sugarcraft cutter
pastry/piping bags, or make
    your own (see page 29)
small, decorative birds

Prepare two quantities of the basic spiced gingerbread as described on page 18, one at a time. Roll each dough into a rounded circle, wrap in clingfilm/plastic wrap and chill for 1–2 hours.

While the dough is resting, cut out the paper templates for making the birdhouse. Lay a sheet of parchment or tracing paper over the outlines on pages 140–41 and trace the shapes needed for the birdhouse walls and roof. Cut out the shapes and write onto each template which shape it corresponds to – this will save confusion later. You will need one paper template for each shape.

Divide each portion of gingerbread dough into three equal pieces, making 6 in total. Dust a work surface and roll out one piece of dough at a time 3 mm/¹/₈ inch thick. Lay each paper template onto a piece of dough and, using a sharp knife, cut around the templates (see picture 1, overleaf). You will need two roof sections, two side walls and two end walls. Carefully arrange them on the prepared baking sheets, allowing plenty of space between each one.

Using the cutter, stamp out one hole from each end wall. Chill for 30 minutes. In the meantime, preheat the oven to 160°C (325°F) Gas 3.

Bake the gingerbread in batches on the middle shelf of the preheated oven for about 10–12 minutes until firm or starting to brown at the edges. Remove from the oven. While the gingerbread is still warm, lay the templates on top of the corresponding shapes and, using a long, sharp knife, trim the edges to neaten them if they have spread slightly during baking. Leave on the sheets to cool completely.

To decorate, warm the jam/jelly to make it runny, then pass it through a sieve/strainer to remove any lumps. Now turn to page 139.

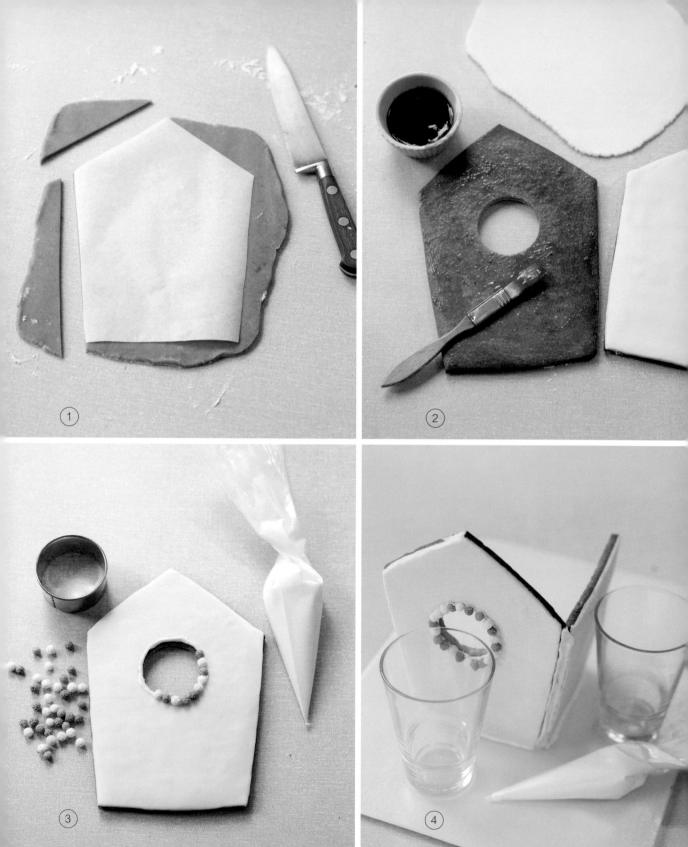

GINGERBREAD BIRDHOUSE DECORATION

Divide the ready-to-roll fondant icing into three equal pieces. Tint one piece red by kneading in a few drops of red food colouring. Tint another piece pale blue and leave the last piece white. Dust the work surface and roll out the red icing to 2 mm/$1/16$ inch thick. Lay the roof template on top of the icing and, using a long knife, cut out two roof shapes.

Lightly brush a little warm jam/jelly over the top of each gingerbread roof tile and gently lay the red icing on top, smoothing into place with your hands and trimming off any excess with scissors or a sharp knife. Repeat with the blue icing for the side walls and the white icing for the end walls. Use the cutter to stamp out the holes in the end walls after you have positioned the icing. (2)

Roll out any white icing off-cuts again and use to stamp out hearts. Brush with a little water and stick them onto the roof Leave to dry for at least two hours.

When you are ready to assemble the birdhouse, it helps to have everything ready and, if possible, a spare pair of hands to hold or pass things as needed. Prepare the royal icing first. Tip the royal icing sugar/mix into a mixing bowl and whisk in 1 teaspoon of cold water at a time to make a smooth icing that is very thick and will hold a stiff peak when the whisk is lifted from the bowl. Spoon the icing into the pastry/piping bag and snip the tip off the bag with scissors so that you can pipe a 2-mm/$1/16$-inch ribbon. Pipe an outline around the round cut-out on each of the end walls and stick the mimosa balls to it. (3)

Taking one side wall, pipe a thick line of icing on the bottom (long) edge and another up one of the short sides and hold this in place, long-side down and gingerbread-side innermost, on one side of a serving plate. This is where the extra hands come in useful. Now take one of the end walls and pipe icing along the bottom (short) edge and one of the side edges. Position this at right angles to the first wall on the plate, with the gingerbread side innermost. Press the two walls together to seal at the corners and hold securely in place for 1–2 minutes until the icing starts to stick.

It is helpful to use glasses or bottles to hold the walls in place while the icing is drying. (4)

Repeat with the second side and end walls – all of the corners should match up and the walls should gently lean outwards. For extra security, pipe more icing on the inside of the wall joins and another neater line on the outside. Leave the glasses or bottles in place against each wall until completely secure – this will take at least 30 minutes and longer to be on the safe side.

When the walls are secure, you are ready to attach the roof. Pipe a thick line of icing along the sloping pitch roof line and along the top of the walls. Taking one roof at a time, hold it in place so that the top of the roof panel lines up with the top of the pitch. Hold this until secure or wedge a glass underneath the roof panel to hold in place while you repeat with the second roof section. Leave to dry for least 30 minutes.

Use the royal icing to stick sugar-paste daisies along the bottom joins of the house, butterflies along the corners of the walls and Smarties/candy-coated chocolates along the top of the roof. Leave to dry for at least 2 hours before arranging the decorative birds in their house.

GINGERBREAD BIRDHOUSE TEMPLATES

To make the Gingerbread Birdhouse on pages 136–9 you will need these templates. Lay a sheet of baking parchment or tracing paper over each outline on these pages, trace the outline, then cut out with scissors. Write onto each template which shape it corresponds to.

ROOF

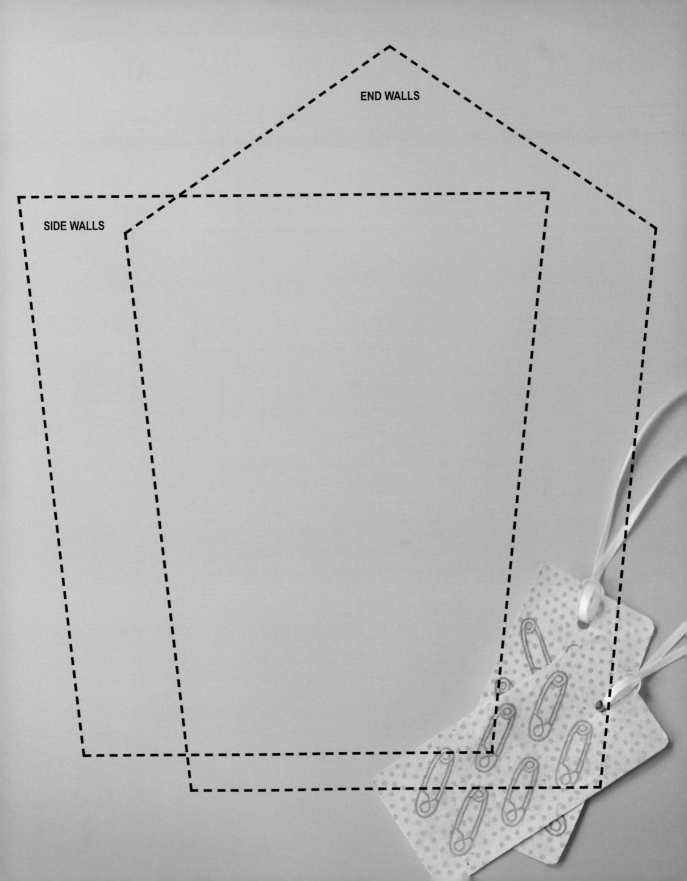

END WALLS

SIDE WALLS

INDEX

Page numbers in *italics* refer to illustrations

PHOTOGRAPHY BY:

Peter Cassidy 90br

Tara Fisher 19, 22, 46, 47, 86–87, 106, 110–111

Laura Forrester 24al

Jonathan Gregson 39

Sandra Lane 3, 10–11, 20–21, 24ar, 31ar & bl, 38, 41, 52, 55, 75, 90l, 93–97, 101, 116–120, 124–127

Adrian Lawrence 27

Lisa Linder 88, 112ar

William Reavell 1, 8, 13, 90ar

Maja Smend 23l, 121

Kate Whitaker 4–5, 14–17, 23r, 24b, 25–26, 28–29, 48br, 64–71, 72a & r, 83–85, 102–105, 109, 112al & b, 114–115, 122–123, 128–141

Claire Winfield 2, 6, 31al, 31br, 33–37, 42–45, 48a & bl, 51, 56–63, 72bl, 76–80, 98, 144, endpapers

BACKGROUND PATTERNS BY:

31 InaKos / Shutterstock.com

49 Sunny Designs / Shutterstock.com

73 Dzmitry Kim / Shutterstock.com

91 Meranda19 / Shutterstock.com

113 atyanaTVK / Shutterstock.com